SECRETS FROM THE BOOK
FOR THE PEOPLE OF THE VALLEY

SECRETS FROM

THE

THE BOOK

FOR THE PEOPLE OF THE VALLEY

J. STEPHEN LANG

with text from *The Book*

TYNDALE HOUSE PUBLISHERS, INC. • WHEATON, ILLINOIS

Visit Tyndale's exciting Web site at www.tyndale.com

Scripture quotations are taken from *The Book*, a special edition of the New Living Translation.

ISBN 0-8423-3915-9

Printed in the United States of America

04 03 02 01 00
5   4   3   2   1

TO

JIM HUNNEWELL

Pastor

Friend

TRUTH is so obscure in these times,

and falsehood so established,

that, unless we love the truth,

we cannot know it.

BLAISE PASCAL

THEN began I with sad and careful heart

to search into the Word of God,

if I could in any place find a word of promise,

or any encouraging sentence,

by which I might take relief.

JOHN BUNYAN

CONTENTS

the PEOPLE of the VALLEY

THE PEOPLE of the Valley had days of sunshine, days of rain. Like most people everywhere, they laughed, they cried, they brought children into the world, they buried the dead, they sang, they danced, they built, they tore down.

Martin was one of the People of the Valley. He had lived in the Valley all his days, as had his father and mother and his grandfathers and grandmothers. He had been taught that there would be joyful days and sad days, and he learned that this was indeed so. He had seen his youth pass, and he had watched his parents grow old. He had seen his own children growing up before his eyes, and he knew he was doing what people do everywhere.

Knowing this pleased Martin. One cool day he was

seated on a hillside, overlooking the houses in the Valley. He looked at his own home, with its smoke curling skyward. He was pleased that he had built a cozy place for his wife and his children and, someday, for his grand-children. He reflected on his joyful days and his sorrowful days and wondered if he had any cause to be bitter. He could think of none, though somehow he felt restless.

Then he thought of his old grandfather, who had died many years before. Before his death, the old man had drawn the young Martin to his side and told him, "Search for the Truth, Martin. Everything else is decoration. Every-thing else in this life is passing, failing, fading away. Search for the Truth, whatever else you do in this life."

And young Martin had promised himself to do this. But he was young, and since no one reminded him of his promise to himself, he forgot the promise.

Now Martin was seated on a hillside, wondering if he had the time or the vigor to keep the promise to himself, wondering if it was worth the trouble after all. But some-thing told him that it *was* worth the trouble.

Martin was looking down upon the houses of the Valley. But something made him turn and look over his shoulder. Suddenly he noticed a traveler he did not know climbing up the back side of the hill. The Unknown Trav-eler carried a walking stick, and in his face he looked weary but determined. Halfway up the hillside he stopped and took a drink from the canteen on his side. Then he paused for a moment, looked carefully at Martin, and proceeded up the hill.

Martin watched the Unknown Traveler. *Perhaps,* Martin thought, *this is one of the buyers who was to call on me today.* But Martin was not in the mood to talk to people about buying and selling. He was thinking about his promise made years ago.

"A lovely day, yes?" said the Unknown Traveler as he stood before Martin. "Cool, but pleasant all in all, wouldn't you say?"

"Pleasant, yes," Martin replied, sizing up the Traveler who stood in front of him. "I don't believe I know you. Are you one of the buyers?"

The Unknown Traveler removed his brown felt hat—its style was not familiar to Martin—dusted it off, and sat down beside Martin. "No, I am no buyer, sir. Just traveling through, you might say. To whom might I have the honor of speaking?"

"My name is Martin. I live here in this Valley. And who are you?"

The Traveler's eyes surveyed the Valley, and Martin could see that he did not intend to answer the question.

"You live in a beautiful place, sir," the Traveler said. "You are grateful, I think, to live in a place not much removed from heaven, yes?"

"Not far from heaven?" Martin replied. "No, indeed, *not* like heaven. People die here, people hurt one another, children grieve their parents, parents grieve their children. I have fallen asleep at the end of a day and said to myself, 'Pity that this glorious day has an ending.' Yet on some nights I have fallen asleep, glad to escape whatever the day's sorrows were. Pain and pleasure, blessing and burden, day after day after day. Good and ill, all mingled together—so, not so much like heaven."

The Unknown Traveler shifted so as to face Martin better. He had intense brown eyes, and he looked directly at Martin as he spoke.

"Were you brought into this world and told you would have only bright days and peaceful nights?"

"No, no one ever told me such a thing. I was prepared for the evil days, though never too pleased when they came. But no one bothered to tell me what it all meant. No one explained why it was worth it, after all was said and done, to live through the good days and the bad days. No one told me I would ever pause as I do today and wonder if I had pursued the right things, loved the right things, looked at this world through the proper lens."

The Unknown Traveler leaned toward Martin as if he were going to tell a great secret. Martin in turn leaned toward him, waiting to hear something he had not heard before.

"Listen," said the Traveler. "You believe you alone are a thinker among the People of the Valley. You think you are the only one wondering about these things. How wrong you are, Martin. The promise you made to yourself years ago was a promise that many others made. But along the way they lost sight of that, and they forgot about the Truth. Now they wonder if it is too late to search, and whether it is worth the while."

Martin did not pause to puzzle over how the Unknown Traveler knew of the promise he had made many years ago. He knew that what the Traveler had said was true, so he saw no point in wondering why or how he knew.

"I am no longer young," Martin said. I have much to keep me busy. My days are full. Promises made in youth cannot always be kept. Still . . ."

"Still, it is important to you. It is more important than any thought that ever was kindled in your head." The Traveler stood, picked up his walking stick, and put on his hat. "Martin, today the Maker of this Valley wants so much for you to remember your promise. He wants everyone to search for the Truth. In fact, he has laid it at your feet, yet you have forgotten it was there." With this the Traveler turned and began climbing down the hill.

"Wait!" Martin shouted as he saw the Traveler moving quickly down the hill. He ran to catch up with him and caught him by the sleeve.

The Traveler turned and gazed into his eyes again. Martin looked like a begging child as he said, "You seem so wise. I wish to talk with you. I would like to keep the promise that I made years ago. You could teach me many things."

"Ah, Martin, no. I have nothing to tell you that you cannot find in The Book."

Martin paused and chewed on his lip for a moment. "The Book?"

"Yes, Martin—think, think back, think long thoughts. You must recall it."

"I remember The Book. I heard my grandparents speak of it years ago. We have it in the Valley somewhere. It's—it's—yes, I remember. It's in a vault underneath the town square."

"Find The Book, Martin. If you want to keep your promise, find The Book. If you seek the Truth, you must begin your search by finding The Book."

"Is The Book—it is the Truth, then?" Martin was pleased that he could find the key to the Truth so quickly, but he distrusted anything that seemed too easy.

"It is the *key* to the Truth. It points to the Truth, and it is rooted in the Truth. The Truth is . . ."

"Yes, yes, tell me. Don't leave me wondering." Martin looked like a small boy, even though his hair was already flecked with gray and his forehead had started to furrow.

"The Truth is not words or thoughts you can define or put a leash on. The Truth is the Creator himself. You meet with the Truth when you meet with him."

"But we can't see the Creator," Martin said anxiously. His eyes were wide with wonder. "I've never heard him speak. I don't know where to find him."

"He reigns."

"That much I believe, yes," Martin said anxiously. "But he does not speak as I now speak with you. So how can I find the Truth, then? If I were to hear his voice . . ."

The Unknown Traveler looked with kindness on Martin. "Listen, Martin. I will teach you something from The Book. What I will tell you is about the Creator, the Truth."

The Traveler paused and looked around the Valley, at its homes and streets. Then he turned again to Martin and spoke these words.

Long ago God spoke many times and in many ways to our ancestors through the prophets. But now in these final days, he has spoken to us through his Son. God promised everything to the Son as an inheritance, and through the Son he made the universe and everything in it. The Son reflects God's own glory, and everything about him represents God exactly.

"Do you understand that, Martin?"

"You are telling me—The Book is telling me—that the Creator has communicated with us through prophets, but that later he spoke through a Son. But what does that Son have to do with The Book?"

"All you know about the Son is to be found in The Book, Martin. If you look for the Truth, look for God. If you look for God, look for the Son. If you look for the Son, open The Book."

The Traveler again started down the hill. Again Martin ran after him. "Wait! I am afraid—afraid that I cannot read The Book even if I find it."

The Traveler stopped and gazed at Martin. "The Book was written for all time, for every man and woman who ever will live. You will understand it. But because you are afraid, I will go with you into the Valley and help you, for now. Come with me, for we haven't much time."

Martin tugged on the sleeve of the Traveler. "Tell me who you are, please."

"That does not matter. You never promised to look for me. You were looking for the Truth. Come with me, let us together find The Book."

FINDING the BOOK

THE PEOPLE of the Valley were not at all surprised by strangers, but somehow the Unknown Traveler who accompanied Martin began to draw their attention. Martin and his new companion walked with the determination of two men on a mission. And though no one in the Valley had ever seen the Traveler, he seemed familiar with every turn in the road. It seemed as though he, not Martin, was leading the way.

The two arrived at the square, where Martin noticed many more people than usual. As he looked about him, he realized that everyone in the Valley was there. Such a thing never happened, not even for the Valley's festivals. But as Martin glanced around, he could not think of a soul he knew who was not there. He was puzzled, and the Traveler puzzled him as well. But his confusion was small compared to his remembrance of his commitment to the Truth.

"Martin," the Traveler said, looking at the rustling poplar leaves as if he knew them well, "you said you could recall where The Book is."

"There is a vault under the gazebo here at the center of the square. See, there are the steps leading down to it." The Traveler could see that the door at the bottom of the steps had not been moved in many a year. Rust was caked about the hinges, and the spiders had done their part to shroud the entrance.

"My grandfather talked about playing in the vault when he was a boy. He said it was a place where the Valley's archives were stored. I suppose the children had enough respect for the Valley's traditions that they could play there without disturbing anything. But no one has been down there for as long as I can remember. Everything down there may have crumbled into dust by now."

"And The Book is down there?"

Martin hesitated, wondering if he had spoken rashly earlier. He had no proof that The Book was anywhere to be found. He had only an old man's memory to go on. Yet something told him The Book was indeed still there.

"I hope it is there. But I don't know who has the key to the vault. And the lock in the door may be too rusty to turn." While he was still speaking the Traveler had descended the steps. He brushed aside the dusty webs and touched the latch on the door. It moved slightly. Then the hinges squealed painfully, and the noise made Martin wince. The Traveler stepped inside the ancient room, and Martin followed him.

Even under decades of dust, the archives were still intact. From what Martin could tell, the books and papers were mostly family histories. Some appeared to be gatherings of laws, and some appeared to be poetry. In one corner of the room was a doll, left long ago by a child who must have seen the place of tradition as a place for play.

The Traveler's eyes surveyed the shelves and tables. Books there were, yet his face showed that his gaze had not yet settled on The Book they had come for. Martin strained his mind, trying to recall whether his grandfather had described to him The Book.

"It was large, I think, and heavy. Its binding was leather, etched with gold. My grandfather said it was beautiful."

"It is indeed," the Traveler said. He reached under a heap of papers underneath a table. When he stood up, he was holding a volume with several layers of dust. It appeared that some of the dust was etched forever into the binding. But when the Traveler blew on the surface, the dust fell away as if it had never belonged there.

The Traveler laid down his walking stick and opened The Book at its center. Then he began to read.

Everything is meaningless, utterly meaningless! Everything is so weary and tiresome!

As I looked at everything I had worked so hard to accomplish, it was all so meaningless. It was like chasing the wind. There was nothing really worthwhile anywhere.

He lifted his eyes from the page and fixed them on Martin's face. "This is an old book, Martin. We are standing here in the midst of oldness. These things here have nothing to say to you, perhaps." And he began to shut The Book. But Martin stopped him.

"No, no, please. Those words—they are not mine, but the heart underneath them is mine. I am a restless man, a wondering man, a man so perplexed by the here and the now that the past does not seem much stranger than the present. Whoever penned those words knew me, or someone like me." Then Martin felt himself a fool for baring his vague anxiety to a stranger. But this passed, and he asked the Traveler, "Is there more in The Book than the sad declarations of the anxious?"

"Indeed, there is more," the Traveler said, and he reopened The Book and read these words.

Listen as wisdom calls out! Hear as understanding raises her voice! She stands on the hilltop and at the crossroads. At the entrance to the city, at the city gates, she cries aloud, "I call to you, to all of you! I am raising my voice to all people. How naive you are! Let me give you common sense. O foolish ones, let me give you understanding. Choose my instruction rather than silver, and knowledge over pure gold.

"The Lord formed me from the beginning, before he created anything else. I was appointed in ages past, at the very first, before the earth began. I was born before the oceans were created, before the springs bubbled forth their waters. Before the mountains and the hills were formed, I was born—before he had made the earth and fields and the first handfuls of soil.

"Listen to my counsel and be wise. Don't ignore it. Happy are those who listen to me, watching for me daily at my gates, waiting for me outside my home! For whoever finds me finds life and wins approval from the Lord. But those who miss me have injured themselves. All who hate me love death."

The Unknown Traveler paused for a moment, and Martin's eyes scanned the page. The words were in his language, yet it seemed as if a mist hung over them, obscuring them. Martin could not tell if the mist was on The Book or in his own eyes. But the Traveler had no trouble reading.

Fear of the Lord is the beginning of wisdom. Knowledge of the Holy One results in understanding.

"This," the Traveler said, "is The Book of God, God who loves the despondent and the perplexed. This is God's Book for Martin and for all seeking the Truth. And you are not the only one, Martin." Then he shut The Book, but Martin was sure he would open it again.

"Come, Martin. It is late in the year. These autumn days are short. Your neighbors are all gathered in the square, and they must hear these words this day." He took up his walking stick and moved toward the steps.

"Wait," Martin said. "They may not listen. This is only an ancient bundle of leather and paper to them. What could the words mean?"

"I cannot promise you that they will listen. I cannot promise you that you will listen further. The Book is not a weapon of coercion. It is The Book of God, and God does not bludgeon people with the Truth. Some will listen, as you did just now. And some will not. And some who listen will not understand, or want to. This is nothing new or strange. Almighty God breathed his life into creatures capable of loving him—or running away. The God of The Book is a risking God."

When Martin heard this, his own doubts were dispelled. He did not know why. He was not sure his neighbors would be so quick to accept The Book. Yet he hoped they would.

The Traveler walked up the steps and into the gazebo. No one had called the People of the Valley together, yet all were there, as if they expected music and dancing in the square. Yet festivity was not in the cool air. Some were there carrying curiosity in their heads, and others carried a readiness to scorn, for there were those who believed that the nagging questions in this life had no real answers. But some were there carrying hope and antic- ipation. And some were there carrying burdens they wished to be rid of.

Martin stepped into the gazebo, believing he would need to introduce the Unknown Traveler to the People of the Valley. But the Traveler stood there as if the whole picture had been painted long before. And Martin joined his neighbors in the square.

"This is The Book of God, God the Father, God who made everything. There is nothing in the world like God. He made this world and reigned over it and treasured it, and he still does so. And long ago he entered it as a man himself. So the lofty One has been where you are—walking on the earth, sweating on humid days, wincing when a splinter pierced his palm, crying over a departed friend, living, feasting, fasting, sorrowing, bleeding, dying."

A few of the older ones nodded, for they could remember hearing of the Son of God who walked the earth. They could remember hearing of this Father who would pour out both discipline and tenderness. Some could even remember hearing of The Book, though this was the first time they had ever seen it.

"The Book is here to disturb you, and to comfort you, and to bring you joy. It is to remind you who God is, and who you are."

As the clouds of October passed their shadows over the Valley's rooftops, the Traveler read these words uttered by the Son of God.

My purpose is to give life in all its fullness.

If you are thirsty, come to me! If you believe in me, come and drink! For the Scriptures declare that rivers of living water will flow out from within.

You will know the truth, and the truth will set you free.

Many of the People of the Valley were thirsty, and many wanted the Truth. And all wanted life in its fullness. So the gates of most hearts there were left ajar.

PAIN
AND
SORROW

SEBASTIAN AND JULIA, who had known much suffering, stood by as they listened to the words from The Book. Sebastian's tired old eyes looked up at the cool gray autumn sky, and he wondered if it might rain. Julia looked at her husband and knew he had seen much pain in life and had come to think there was no hope for it. Though she was a shy and timid woman by nature, she stepped forward and, trembling a little, spoke to the Unknown Traveler.

"Sir, you tell us about the Creator who made this world and everything in it. I believe in that Creator, and so does my poor husband here. But we have known so much hurt. Our children are all dead. We have lost almost everything we owned at one time. So many times we have suffered in sickness. Tell us, if there is anything good to tell, about sorrow."

The Unknown Traveler looked for a long time into Julia's tired old eyes. A tiny tear rolled down his cheek, but then he smiled, as if he knew he could give her what she had asked for. Then he lifted up The Book and began to speak.

The Lord is close to the brokenhearted; he rescues those who are crushed in spirit.

The righteous face many troubles, but the Lord rescues them from each and every one.

He heals the brokenhearted, binding up their wounds.

We are pressed on every side by troubles, but we are not crushed and broken. We are perplexed, but we don't give up and quit. We are hunted down, but God never abandons us. We get knocked down, but we get up again and keep going.

That is why we never give up. Though our bodies are dying, our spirits are being renewed every day. For our present troubles are quite small and won't last very long. Yet they produce for us an immeasurably great glory that will last forever!

So we don't look at the troubles we can see right now; rather, we look forward to what we have not yet seen. For the troubles we see will soon be over, but the joys to come will last forever.

No matter what happens, always be thankful, for this is God's will for you who belong to Christ Jesus.

Martin was listening closely. He remembered a cold night many years ago when the home of Sebastian and Julia burned to the foundation. Looking at Sebastian's face now, he could recall the shadows cast by the leaping flames on the man's bewildered countenance. And Julia's shrieking still echoed inside him. No one in the Valley would ever forget her frenzy over her daughter's death in the fire. Then the Traveler began to read again.

The steps of the godly are directed by the Lord. He delights in every detail of their lives. Though they stumble, they will not fall, for the Lord holds them by the hand.

He will never abandon the godly. He will keep them safe forever.

"For I know the plans I have for you," says the Lord. "they are plans for good and not for disaster, to give you a future and a hope. In those days when you pray, I will listen. If you look for me in earnest, you will find me when you seek me."

The Unknown Traveler looked around at the People of the Valley and knew that many of them had known much heartache. In some faces were marks of weariness

and woe, in some only bitterness. And in some was the
bland lukewarmness of resignation. He pitied these most,
for they bore the twin burden of wearisome yesterdays and
new days that would only reprise the old. Again he lifted
up The Book and began to speak. "Listen, people, to what
a man of sorrow said about his God."

I waited patiently for the Lord to help me, and he
turned to me and heard my cry. He lifted me out of
the pit of despair, out of the mud and the mire. He
set my feet on solid ground and steadied me as I
walked along. He has given me a new song to sing, a
hymn of praise to our God. Many will see what he
has done and be astounded. They will put their trust
in the Lord.

Then the Traveler said, "Now listen to the words of
another man who suffered much."

You have allowed me to suffer much hardship.
    You keep track of all my sorrows. You have
collected all my tears in your bottle. You have
recorded each one in your book.
    But you will restore me to life again and lift me up
from the depths of the earth. You will restore me to
even greater honor and comfort me once again.
    O God, I praise your word. Yes, Lord, I praise your

word. I trust in God, so why should I be afraid? What can mere mortals do to me?

This I know: God is on my side.

Sebastian and Julia smiled a little, glad to know that the God who gave The Book to them cared for those who were hurting. The Unknown Traveler began to speak again, for he wanted them to know that the Son of God, God in the flesh, was filled with compassion for the burdened ones.

Jesus said, "Come to me, all of you who are weary and carry heavy burdens, and I will give you rest. Take my yoke upon you. Let me teach you, because I am humble and gentle, and you will find rest for your souls. For my yoke fits perfectly, and the burden I give you is light."

Then the Unknown Traveler paused and said, "Do you hesitate to believe this? Listen to one who remembered the good days in the midst of bad days."

I know how to live on almost nothing or with everything. I have learned the secret of living in every situation, whether it is with a full stomach or empty, with plenty or little. For I can do everything with the help of Christ who gives me the strength I need.

We know that God causes everything to work together for the good of those who love God and are called according to his purpose for them.

If God is for us, who can ever be against us?

The Traveler paused and spoke to them, his words settling upon them like the sweet and familiar breath of an old companion filled with compassion yet bent on telling the truth.

"You were placed in this beautiful theater to act out your part as stewards of the earth and worshipers of God. And your great failing is the same one that century after century raises up walls between the Loving One and his creatures—their yearning to worship someone else, something else, anything else but the One who merits worship. Some worship their past and their pain, paying hourly homage to it, kneeling before it, offering up their fractured hearts on it, singing hymns to their hurts. Their pain becomes a temple 'round itself, and they become the devotees of anguish. They forget that some of the sweetest anthems ever sung have poured out of those whose hearts were spent. They forget that joy comes, sometimes slowly, but eventually, inevitably, for those who love Almighty God more than their all-consuming afflictions."

When old Sebastian heard these words, he knew the Traveler was one who could speak healing words. Then the

Traveler began to read again, words of comfort that had fountained out of one who loved God more than his woes.

> I know the Lord is always with me. I will not be shaken, for he is right beside me.
>
> No wonder my heart is filled with joy!
>
> I will praise the Lord at all times. I will constantly speak his praises. Let all who are discouraged take heart.

The Traveler stopped reading and slowly closed The Book. But Martin and some of the others looked at him with the wide eyes of hungry children who have just had morsels of warm bread dropped into their quivering palms. Martin, like all the other People of the Valley, was capable of selfishness, yet sympathy sometimes wrapped itself about him as if begging him to look outward at another creature's anguish. And he had lived too long in this Valley not to have hurt along with his neighbors. So, like a cool hand upon the fevered brow, the Traveler soothingly pressed these words upon them.

> The Lord is my light and my salvation—so why should I be afraid? The Lord protects me from danger—so why should I tremble? When evil people come to destroy me, when my enemies and foes attack me, they will stumble and fall. Though a

mighty army surrounds me, my heart will know no fear. Even if they attack me, I remain confident.

I prayed to the Lord, and he answered me, freeing me from all my fears.

Praise the Lord, I tell myself; with my whole heart, I will praise his holy name. Praise the Lord, I tell myself, and never forget the good things he does for me. He surrounds me with love and tender mercies. He fills my life with good things. My youth is renewed like the eagle's!

The Lord is like a father to his children, tender and compassionate to those who fear him.

A woman in the square winced as she heard these words about the loving Father, for her own father had mingled embraces with bruises. The same hands that stroked the child's face blackened it, and the memories crouched inside her like sullen beasts.

The Traveler saw from her posture and her expression that she wanted not only healing but a father. "Listen," the Traveler said, "to the comfort this Father gives his children."

Don't be afraid, for I am with you. Do not be dismayed, for I am your God. I will strengthen you. I will help you. I will uphold you with my victorious right hand.

I am holding you by your right hand—I, the Lord your God. And I say to you, 'Do not be afraid. I am here to help you. Despised though you are, don't be afraid, for I will help you. I am the Lord, your Redeemer. I am the Holy One.

When the poor and needy search for water and there is none, and their tongues are parched from thirst, then I, the Lord, will answer them. I will never forsake them.

When you go through deep waters and great trouble, I will be with you. When you go through rivers of difficulty, you will not drown! When you walk through the fire of oppression, you will not be burned up; the flames will not consume you.

Because you trusted me, I will preserve your life and keep you safe. I, the Lord, have spoken!

Old Sebastian stepped forward and said quietly, "Does this loving Father really care for us? I believe, yet I want to hear it over and over again. Please, speak to us more about the love he has for those who grieve."

Then the Unknown Traveler set down The Book and spoke words from it that he seemed to know by heart.

Be still in the presence of the Lord, and wait patiently for him to act. Those who trust in the Lord will possess the land.

So it is good to wait quietly for salvation from the Lord.

We can rejoice, too, when we run into problems and trials, for we know that they are good for us— they help us learn to endure. And endurance develops strength of character in us, and character strengthens our confident expectation of salvation.

But if we look forward to something we don't have yet, we must wait patiently and confidently.

For when your faith is tested, your endurance has a chance to grow. So let it grow, for when your endurance is fully developed, you will be strong in character and ready for anything.

God is our refuge and strength, always ready to help in times of trouble. So we will not fear, even if earthquakes come and the mountains crumble into the sea.

Then the Unknown Traveler heard the sound of a broken man weeping, and he knew that men could still weep because they had heard good things.

FORGIVENESS
AND
MERCY

CLARICE, a young woman who held a grudge against her sister, had listened to the words from The Book. Under the cool autumn sky she shivered, but not from the autumn breeze. She shivered as someone shivers when hearing something painfully but beautifully true.

Yet she felt inside herself a certain hardness. She wondered if anything could ever remove that hardness. She wondered if she could ever learn how to forgive.

She had never been a bold woman, but she stepped forward, and, almost murmuring, she spoke to the Unknown Traveler.

"You say things about the Maker of this world that touch me. I believe he must be great and mighty, a Maker of wondrous things. I believe he could transform an empty blackness into the universe. But could this same Maker show me how to heal a gap between one sister and another? How can we forgive each other?"

The Unknown Traveler knew that he could tell this woman about forgiveness by speaking of the forgiveness of a wayward son.

A man had two sons. The younger son told his father, "I want my share of your estate now, instead of waiting until you die." So his father agreed to divide his wealth between his sons.

A few days later this younger son packed all his belongings and took a trip to a distant land, and there he wasted all his money on wild living. About the time his money ran out, a great famine swept over the land, and he began to starve. He persuaded a local farmer to hire him to feed his pigs. The boy became so hungry that even the pods he was feeding the pigs looked good to him. But no one gave him anything.

When he finally came to his senses, he said to himself, "At home even the hired men have food enough to spare, and here I am, dying of hunger! I will go home to my father and say, 'Father, I have sinned against both heaven and you, and I am no longer worthy of being called your son. Please take me on as a hired man.'"

So he returned home to his father. And while he was still a long distance away, his father saw him coming. Filled with love and compassion, he ran to his son, embraced him, and kissed him. His son said to him, "Father, I have sinned against both heaven and you, and I am no longer worthy of being called your son."

But his father said to the servants, "Quick! Bring the finest robe in the house and put it on him. Get a ring for his finger, and sandals for his feet. And kill the calf we have been fattening in the pen. We must celebrate with a feast, for this son of mine was dead and has now returned to life. He was lost, but now he is found." So the party began.

Then the Traveler read another story about the need to forgive.

The Kingdom of Heaven can be compared to a king who decided to bring his accounts up to date with servants who had borrowed money from him. In the process, one of his debtors was brought in who owed him millions of dollars. He couldn't pay, so the king ordered that he, his wife, his children, and everything he had be sold to pay the debt. But the man fell down before the king and begged him, "Oh, sir, be patient with me, and I will pay it all." Then the king was filled with pity for him, and he released him and forgave his debt.

But when the man left the king, he went to a fellow servant who owed him a few thousand dollars. He grabbed him by the throat and demanded instant payment. His fellow servant fell down before him and begged for a little more time. "Be patient and I will pay it," he pleaded. But his creditor wouldn't wait. He had the man arrested and jailed until the debt could be paid in full.

When some of the other servants saw this, they were very upset. They went to the king and told him what had happened. Then the king called in the man he had forgiven and said, "You evil servant! I forgave you that tremendous debt because you pleaded with me. Shouldn't you have mercy on your fellow servant, just as I had mercy on you?" Then the angry king sent the man to prison until he had paid every penny.

That's what my heavenly Father will do to you if you refuse to forgive your brothers and sisters in your heart.

Clarice listened closely to the story. So did Martin, who also had known the bitterness that comes from not forgiving.

The Unknown Traveler continued to read.

If you forgive those who sin against you, your heavenly Father will forgive you. But if you refuse to forgive others, your Father will not forgive your sins.

When you are praying, first forgive anyone you are holding a grudge against, so that your Father in heaven will forgive your sins, too.

You must make allowance for each other's faults and forgive the person who offends you. Remember, the Lord forgave you, so you must forgive others.

Don't repay evil for evil. Don't retaliate when people say unkind things about you. Instead, pay them back with a blessing. That is what God wants you to do, and he will bless you for it.

Do not rejoice when your enemies fall into trouble. Don't be happy when they stumble.

And don't say, "Now I can pay them back for all their meanness to me! I'll get even!"

If your enemies are hungry, give them food to eat. If they are thirsty, give them water to drink.

Dear friends, never avenge yourselves. Leave that to God. For it is written, "I will take vengeance; I will repay those who deserve it," says the Lord. Don't let evil get the best of you, but conquer evil by doing good.

Don't resist an evil person! If you are slapped on the right cheek, turn the other, too. If you are

ordered to court and your shirt is taken from you,
give your coat, too.

"You understand all of this, don't you?" asked the
Unknown Traveler. "These truths are so simple. Think of
how you could summarize them all." Then he began to
read again from The Book.

God blesses those who are merciful, for they will be
shown mercy.
Be kind to each other, tenderhearted, forgiving
one another, just as God through Christ has forgiven
you.

"You see," said the Traveler, "there is unbounded
forgiveness for you. There are no limits on it at all. Once
the Son of God had a question posed to him about whether
there were indeed limits to forgiveness."

Then Peter came to him and asked, "Lord, how often
should I forgive someone who sins against me? Seven
times?"
"No!" Jesus replied, "seventy times seven!"

"How hard this seems," the Traveler said, "yet it's so
simple, really. But you must know that people always suffer
for living the truth. So remember these words."

If people persecute you because you are a Christian, don't curse them; pray that God will bless them.

Never pay back evil for evil to anyone. Do things in such a way that everyone can see you are honorable.

"I have one more thing to read," said the Unknown Traveler. "It is something you should hope you will be able to say about yourselves someday. Listen closely."

We bless those who curse us. We are patient with those who abuse us. We respond gently when evil things are said about us.

Then Clarice closed her eyes and resolved to believe the Truth and do the Truth. And she no longer shivered, though the cool breeze blew through the willows on the square.

LOVE

AS A MILD breeze of autumn passed lazily over the square, some of the people pulled their wraps around them. It was late in the season, and the breeze was now of the shivering kind.

But one young couple, so taken with each other that they could scarce bear to shift their gaze from each other to the Unknown Traveler, did not feel the breeze at all, so warmed were they by the fire they had kindled in themselves.

The girl, though, had heard some of the Traveler's words, and without fully taking her eyes from the boy, said to the Traveler, "Love is the greatest thing in the world, is it not? Tell us more about love."

"Greatest, grandest, noblest, purest—how many

words and images we could pile one on another, yet we would not do it justice," said the Unknown Traveler. "In truth, there are no words to define it. It is defined only by the source, God, and the Son of God. We know nothing of love unless we know of them."

Then he began to read from The Book.

The Lord is like a father to his children, tender and compassionate to those who fear him. For he understands how weak we are; he knows we are only dust. Our days on earth are like grass; like wildflowers, we bloom and die. The wind blows, and we are gone—as though we had never been here. But the love of the Lord remains forever with those who fear him.

God showed his great love for us by sending Christ to die for us while we were still sinners.

God is so rich in mercy, and he loved us so very much, that even while we were dead because of our sins, he gave us life when he raised Christ from the dead. (It is only by God's special favor that you have been saved!) For he raised us from the dead along with Christ, and we are seated with him in the heavenly realms—all because we are one with Christ Jesus.

God our Savior showed us his kindness and love. He saved us, not because of the good things we did, but because of his mercy. He washed away our sins and gave us a new life through the Holy Spirit. He generously poured out the Spirit upon us because of what Jesus Christ our Savior did.

God showed how much he loved us by sending his only Son into the world so that we might have eternal life through him. This is real love. It is not that we loved God, but that he loved us and sent his Son as a sacrifice to take away our sins.

Some among the People of the Valley were puzzled by what the Traveler said about Jesus, the Son of God. But a few remembered hearing of how he had taught marvelous things, healed the sick, and then died like a criminal so that all people, though failing to live as God had intended, would not have to die eternally. And the ones who remembered these things hoped that the Traveler would soon say more. Then the Traveler spoke to the young couple again.

"Ah, young ones, you stand there in the chill of autumn gleaming like stars, and seeing you is itself a delight. You will always remember these glory days, remember how the swan in the evening moved over the lake as you stood there at the water's edge, believing no two people had beheld such a sunset.

"Yet how much you have to learn of love, for the enchantment and the ardor wane when love is rooted in what we think is lovable. How quick we are to smile on what charms us, how quick to express our love for it. Yet the love of the Creator of this fallen world goes so much beyond that, for he showed that love is best when it is bestowed on what is not lovable. Page after page of The Book testifies to that kind of love, the love of a righteous God for people who are not righteous."

Then he began to read again, so they would know how to respond to the love they did not deserve from God.

> You must love the Lord your God with all your heart, all your soul, and all your strength.
>
> What does the Lord your God require of you? He requires you to fear him, to live according to his will, to love and worship him with all your heart and soul, and to obey the Lord's commands and laws that I am giving you today for your own good.
>
> The Lord has already told you what is good, and this is what he requires: to do what is right, to love mercy, and to walk humbly with your God.
>
> Love the Lord your God, walk in all his ways, obey his commands, be faithful to him, and serve him with all your heart and all your soul.
>
> Take delight in the Lord, and he will give you your heart's desires.
>
> Love the Lord, all you faithful ones! For the Lord protects those who are loyal to him, but he harshly punishes all who are arrogant.

Seeing again the young couple, and knowing they would often murmur tender words to each other, the Traveler read these words of those whose love for God had erupted into song.

I love you, Lord; you are my strength.

Whom have I in heaven but you? I desire you more than anything on earth. My health may fail, and my spirit may grow weak, but God remains the strength of my heart; he is mine forever.

How I delight in your commands! How I love them! I honor and love your commands. I meditate on your principles.

Even perfection has its limits, but your commands have no limit. Oh, how I love your law! I think about it all day long.

I love the Lord because he hears and answers my prayers. Because he bends down and listens, I will pray as long as I have breath!

Cecilia, a woman not far past the prime of life, had long ago forgotten how to love her husband, and he had given her the same gift of unkindness. The woman could see the young couple standing there, and in her bitterness she did as the bitter often do and uttered words of painful truth.

"Sir," she said to the Traveler, "we have all known lovers so lost in their own universe that they cared for no one else. And we have all known people who claimed to be worshipers of God, yet these same people cared for no one besides those in their own circle. Is God pleased when people sing of their devotion to him and sneer at those around them?"

The Traveler knew that the woman already knew the answer to her question. Yet her words deserved a longer answer from The Book, and so he gave it to her.

Let love be your highest goal.

Love your neighbor as yourself.

Love means doing what God has commanded us, and he has commanded us to love one another, just as you heard from the beginning.

Dear friends, let us continue to love one another, for love comes from God. Anyone who loves is born of God and knows God. But anyone who does not love does not know God—for God is love.

Dear friends, since God loved us that much, we surely ought to love each other. No one has ever seen God. But if we love each other, God lives in us, and his love has been brought to full expression through us.

And God has given us his Spirit as proof that we live in him and he in us. Furthermore, we have seen with our own eyes and now testify that the Father sent his Son to be the Savior of the world. All who

proclaim that Jesus is the Son of God have God
living in them, and they live in God.

Now you can have sincere love for each other as
brothers and sisters because you were cleansed from
your sins when you accepted the truth of the Good
News. So see to it that you really do love each other
intensely with all your hearts.

Don't just pretend that you love others. Really
love them. Hate what is wrong. Stand on the side of
the good. Love each other with genuine affection,
and take delight in honoring each other.

Anyone who hates a Christian brother or sister is
living and walking in darkness. Such a person is lost,
having been blinded by the darkness.

The Traveler looked at Cecilia, the bitter woman,
then at the young couple. "How unlike the way of this selfish world, to love one who is not lovable. When someone's
face or heart is pleasing to you, you are drawn toward it
like one who hears celestial music coming from behind a
door. You will always want to open that door, wanting to
be closer, to find love. But behind another door you hear
discord, or foreign music that seems strange to you, and you
walk the other way. Yet those doors, too, must be opened."

All of you should be of one mind, full of sympathy
toward each other, loving one another with tender

hearts and humble minds. Don't repay evil for evil. Don't retaliate when people say unkind things about you. Instead, pay them back with a blessing. That is what God wants you to do, and he will bless you for it.

Pay all your debts, except the debt of love for others. You can never finish paying that! If you love your neighbor, you will fulfill all the requirements of God's law. For the commandments against adultery and murder and stealing and coveting—and any other commandment—are all summed up in this one commandment: "Love your neighbor as yourself."

We know how much God loves us, and we have put our trust in him.

God is love, and all who live in love live in God, and God lives in them. And as we live in God, our love grows more perfect. So we will not be afraid on the day of judgment, but we can face him with confidence because we are like Christ here in this world.

Love does no wrong to anyone, so love satisfies all of God's requirements.

Because the Traveler knew that loving others was painful and demanding, he continued with painful words.

Do you think you deserve credit merely for loving those who love you? Even the sinners do that! And if you do good only to those who do good to you, is that so wonderful? Even sinners do that much! And if you lend money only to those who can repay you, what good is that? Even sinners will lend to their own kind for a full return.

Love your enemies! Do good to them! Lend to them! And don't be concerned that they might not repay. Then your reward from heaven will be very great, and you will truly be acting as children of the Most High, for he is kind to the unthankful and to those who are wicked.

"Dear friends," the Traveler said, "some of your teachers have told you of animals and how they appear to show kindness to one another. And this is so, for the One who set the world in motion and holds its particles together—he infused his order with not only harmony but also charity. But know this: No beast and no bird spreads out a feast for its enemies. The murderer may one day dine with the father of his victim, because the father can forgive, as any man can. No creature can do such things, none but the man whose heart beats like the heart of God, pulsing with those living words *I forgive; I love; I forgive; I love*. The beasts do not sin, but the beasts do not—cannot—forgive. And so they do not know fully the love of the forgiver for the forgiven."

Then the Traveler read again.

Since God chose you to be the holy people whom he loves, you must clothe yourselves with tenderhearted mercy, kindness, humility, gentleness, and patience. You must make allowance for each other's faults and forgive the person who offends you. Remember, the Lord forgave you, so you must forgive others.

You must be compassionate, just as your Father is compassionate.

Anyone who loves other Christians is living in the light and does not cause anyone to stumble.

And so God can always point to us as examples of the incredible wealth of his favor and kindness toward us, as shown in all he has done for us through Christ Jesus.

Martin was deeply moved by all the Traveler had said. "What you said before is true, Traveler. You said that love lies beyond all words. There is nothing more that could be said about it."

"Friend, you are right," the Traveler responded. "Yet like all that is inexpressible, the ones who have encountered it will never hesitate to find the words to express it. And perhaps the greatest words of all are these, written by one who knew how frail and empty words could be." And with that he began to read again.

If I could speak in any language in heaven or on earth but didn't love others, I would only be making meaningless noise like a loud gong or a clanging cymbal. If I had the gift of prophecy, and if I knew all the mysteries of the future and knew everything about everything, but didn't love others, what good would I be? And if I had the gift of faith so that I could speak to a mountain and make it move, without love I would be no good to anybody.

Love is patient and kind. Love is not jealous or boastful or proud or rude. Love does not demand its own way. Love is not irritable, and it keeps no record of when it has been wronged. It is never glad about injustice but rejoices whenever the truth wins out. Love never gives up, never loses faith, is always hopeful, and endures through every circumstance.

Love will last forever, but prophecy and speaking in tongues and special knowledge will all disappear. For even our special knowledge is incomplete, and our prophecy is incomplete. But when the end comes, these special gifts will all disappear.

There are three things that will endure—faith, hope, and love—and the greatest of these is love.

And the most important piece of clothing you must wear is love. Love is what binds us all together in perfect harmony.

And with that he closed The Book for a while, for it did not now seem right to speak anymore.

FRIENDSHIP

JARED AND EDMUND had been friends since boyhood. Now the two of them stood in the square, their hair much whiter and thinner than it was decades ago when they scrambled up the old mulberry trees in the Valley, giggling like fools, unashamed of their merriment.

But today the two were not standing together. They were on opposite sides of the square, and once when their eyes met they both looked away. The two old friends had quarreled weeks and weeks ago, and though the memory of the quarrel was fading, the bitter resentment that abides after quarrels was still there, lingering like the sullen smoke that hangs after a great fire has long passed.

For such as these—people who had known ironclad

love and were willing to throw it aside—the Traveler
began to read from The Book.

> After David had finished talking with Saul, he met
> Jonathan, the king's son. There was an immediate
> bond of love between them, and they became the
> best of friends.
>
> And Jonathan made David reaffirm his vow of
> friendship again, for Jonathan loved David as much
> as he loved himself.

"Dear people," the Traveler said, looking with
compassion on Jared, "you may go to your graves debat-
ing the nature of love. But how often in the history of
this tired, erring world has there ever been a love that
endured and matured better than the best of friend-
ships? The fiery love that takes possession of man and
woman—what a delight it is while it burns! What joy
in gazing into the eyes of another! Yet what compares
with two pairs of eyes gazing in the same direction,
fixed on the same goal? What compares with Jonathan,
the king of Israel's noble son, and his love for David,
the king-to-be? Does not every wife yearn for her
husband to love her with such unwearying love? Hear
the words of a man with his heart in tatters over a
friend who died."

How I weep for you, my brother Jonathan! Oh, how much I loved you! And your love for me was deep, deeper than the love of women!

Many of the People of the Valley had known Jared and Edmund for years, and the two men's quarrel was a thing for gossips to feed on. But no one who heard the Traveler's words could help but feel for the two old men and the love that had seen them through sunshine and shadow, fountains of laughter and torrents of tears. And the two old men themselves ached as the Traveler began to read again.

A friend is always loyal, and a brother is born to help in time of need.

Wounds from a friend are better than many kisses from an enemy.

The heartfelt counsel of a friend is as sweet as perfume and incense.

As iron sharpens iron, a friend sharpens a friend.

Edmund's son was standing near his father, and he leaned forward and began to whisper in his ear. "Father, I don't understand this senseless argument you've had." But before he could say more, the old man hushed him with a firm wave of his hand. Edmund was listening to the Traveler, but his pride gripped him and murmured, "Wait, wait, and let the offending party make the first step toward reconciling." And as men love to listen to pride, Edmund listened. Yet he was not sure who the offending party was, himself or Jared, or whether it mattered at all.

Then the Unknown Traveler read these words about the peculiar efficiency of love.

Two people can accomplish more than twice as much as one; they get a better return for their labor. If one person falls, the other can reach out and help. But people who are alone when they fall are in real trouble.

And on a cold night, two under the same blanket can gain warmth from each other. But how can one be warm alone?

A person standing alone can be attacked and defeated, but two can stand back-to-back and conquer. Three are even better, for a triple-braided cord is not easily broken.

The Traveler looked at Edmund's face, which was now set like a stone, made stern by pride. Then he read these words.

Hatred stirs up quarrels, but love covers all offenses.

Disregarding another person's faults preserves love; telling about them separates close friends.

How wonderful it is, how pleasant, when brothers live together in harmony!

Never abandon a friend—either yours or your father's.

Love each other with genuine affection, and take delight in honoring each other.

Then Jared marveled in his heart that he and his companion of so many decades had so quickly forgotten how to honor each other. Jared was old, and he remembered his aged father speaking these words from The Book.

One should be kind to a fainting friend.

And, ah, how often the constant Edmund had proved himself to be kind.

Then Jared recalled these other words his father had said to him.

There are "friends" who destroy each other, but a real friend sticks closer than a brother.

Jared had never regretted having Edmund by his side. For in more than seventy years of life he had had friends richer, more influential, more learned, quicker of wit, more well-appointed in their dress, more gracious in their manner. But never had he taken a more loyal man to his heart. And as he came to know loyalty by seeing loyalty, others saw the two of them as a standard of loyalty. So his father's words—the words from The Book—had been proved true. Anyone who knew Jared would know what Edmund was like, and those who knew Edmund knew Jared. And to know either was to know fidelity.

Then Jared remembered, as the aged so easily remember words spoken in their childhood, other words from The Book. But these were the words of a man whose friends had failed him when he was in the dust.

> My friends scorn me, but I pour out my tears to God. Oh, that someone would mediate between God and me, as a person mediates between friends.

And Jared pitied that poor man, for he knew that he could not endure Edmund scoffing at him. But this had never happened, and for this he was thankful.

As a tiny bead of shame dropped onto the two men's pride and began to erode it like acid, the Traveler read these words spoken by the Son of God to his beloved disciples.

> I command you to love each other in the same way that I love you. And here is how to measure it—the greatest love is shown when people lay down their lives for their friends.

And while some of the People of the Valley puzzled at these words, knowing how uncommon it must be for anyone to show so much love, Jared and Edmund considered that they had both known, in each other, such a man. And though neither had ever been called to lay down his life for the other, neither doubted that it could be done if it must be done.

Stubbornness is a force based on folly, and when folly is seen for what it is, the stubbornness gladly melts. And pride, diamond-hard though it is, gives way meekly to love, which in the end is harder than anything else, though its outside is supple and warm.

When the Traveler looked at the spot where Jared had been standing, no one was there. Edmund, likewise, was not where he had been. And in the mass of people there they could not be seen for the time being. But the Traveler did not doubt that in only a moment the two would be drawing very near to each other.

Some of the People of the Valley pondered the words the Son of God had said to his well-loved followers. And some began to understand what a great compliment had been paid to those disciples.

MARRIAGE

A COUPLE many years married, Clement and Lenore, stood side by side in the square as the Unknown Traveler spoke. He could tell from looking at them that they had lived many days and nights together, sharing words of compassion and fondness, but also sharing words that cut like daggers. And he knew that other husbands and wives had likewise learned to wound with words and with looks. So the Traveler began to speak The Book's words about why a man and woman would ever want to join together for life.

> The Lord God said, "It is not good for the man to be alone. I will make a companion who will help him." So the Lord God formed from the soil every kind of

animal and bird. He brought them to Adam to see what he would call them, and Adam chose a name for each one. He gave names to all the livestock, birds, and wild animals. But still there was no companion suitable for him.

So the Lord God caused Adam to fall into a deep sleep. He took one of Adam's ribs and closed up the place from which he had taken it. Then the Lord God made a woman from the rib and brought her to Adam.

"At last!" Adam exclaimed. "She is part of my own flesh and bone! She will be called 'woman,' because she was taken out of a man." This explains why a man leaves his father and mother and is joined to his wife, and the two are united into one.

In relationships among the Lord's people, women are not independent of men, and men are not independent of women.

The Traveler could tell from Clement's tired eyes that he understood the words. Yet Clement's face also showed that he had long ago ceased to see his wife as a good companion. And Lenore, too, showed in her face that her early love had faded. Then the Traveler spoke again, looking intently at the women in the square.

The man who finds a wife finds a treasure and receives favor from the Lord.

A worthy wife is her husband's joy and crown; a shameful wife saps his strength.

In the same way, you wives must accept the authority of your husbands, even those who refuse to accept the Good News. Your godly lives will speak to them better than any words. They will be won over.

For instance, Sarah obeyed her husband, Abraham, when she called him her master. You are her daughters when you do what is right without fear of what your husbands might do.

Charm is deceptive, and beauty does not last; but a woman who fears the Lord will be greatly praised.

Don't be concerned about the outward beauty that depends on fancy hairstyles, expensive jewelry, or beautiful clothes. You should be known for the beauty that comes from within, the unfading beauty of a gentle and quiet spirit, which is so precious to God. That is the way the holy women of old made themselves beautiful. They trusted God and accepted the authority of their husbands.

As he spoke, Lenore remembered how their home, so peaceful in the early years of a long marriage, had so often seemed like a battleground. She remembered the part she had played in the strife. And the Traveler's words cut her, though it was the kind of cut that brings healing.

The Traveler spoke again, looking first at Clement,

then at many of the other men gathered there, knowing that they had forgotten the gentleness of their younger days.

> Live happily with the woman you love through all the meaningless days of life that God has given you in this world. The wife God gives you is your reward for all your earthly toil.
>
> Drink water from your own well—share your love only with your wife.
>
> Let your wife be a fountain of blessing for you. Rejoice in the wife of your youth. She is a loving doe, a graceful deer. May you always be captivated by her love.
>
> Each man must love his wife as he loves himself, and the wife must respect her husband.
>
> You husbands must give honor to your wives. Treat her with understanding as you live together. She may be weaker than you are, but she is your equal partner in God's gift of new life. If you don't treat her as you should, your prayers will not be heard.
>
> You husbands must love your wives with the same love Christ showed the church. He gave up his life for her.

There were also in the crowd two people, a husband and a wife, who were not standing side by side. The husband, Nicholas, and the wife, Monica, had abandoned all hope for their marriage. The vows they had made when their young eyes had shimmered with love were now regarded as a hindrance. They intended to dissolve what they had once sworn could never be dissolved. And while they thought of divorce, they were not the only couple to think this way. This the Traveler knew, for it was true everywhere. So he spoke these words to the People of the Valley.

Didn't the Lord make you one with your wife? In body and spirit you are his. And what does he want? Godly children from your union. So guard yourself; remain loyal to the wife of your youth. "For I hate divorce!" says the Lord, the God of Israel.

But God's plan was seen from the beginning of creation, for "He made them male and female." This explains why a man leaves his father and mother and is joined to his wife, and the two are united into one. Since they are no longer two but one, let no one separate them, for God has joined them together.

When Jesus was alone with his disciples in the house, they brought up the subject again. He told them, "Whoever divorces his wife and marries someone else commits adultery against her. And if a woman divorces her husband and remarries, she commits adultery."

At this last word one woman winced, though she knew the husband she loved so dearly would never divorce her. But she knew that he had come to scoff at his vow of fidelity. And a wave of pain washed over her. Then the Traveler spoke.

Give honor to marriage, and remain faithful to one another in marriage. God will surely judge people who are immoral and those who commit adultery.

Why be captivated, my son, with an immoral woman, or embrace the breasts of an adulterous woman? For the Lord sees clearly what a man does, examining every path he takes.

One young man, a tall, bearded scholar, stood by, nodding his head in agreement, for he had seen people wounded by divorce. And though he knew the pains of unhappy homes where marriage had become lifeless and empty, he knew also of the bitterness of marriage dissolved. He had even asked himself many times if perhaps it might be best not to marry at all. But the fear of living alone in a world of married couples gnawed at him. His eyes widened as the Traveler began to speak again.

Yes, it is good to live a celibate life. But because there is so much sexual immorality, each man should have his own wife, and each woman should have her own husband.

This is only my suggestion. It's not meant to be an absolute rule. I wish everyone could get along without marrying, just as I do. But we are not all the same. God gives some the gift of marriage, and to others he gives the gift of singleness.

I am saying this for your benefit, not to place restrictions on you. I want you to do whatever will help you serve the Lord best, with as few distractions as possible.

The young man heard these words and took comfort in knowing that he could please God whether he chose to marry or not.

As the Traveler looked around the square, he could see the faces of eager youth, some of them anticipating the joys of marriage, some of them already sure that marriage would inevitably lapse into a tedious ritual, to be followed by other marriages that would also fade and fail. The Traveler could see older couples whose lives had indeed become tedious. Yet his gaze rested for a time on one elderly couple that seemed almost to be looking at him with the same pair of eyes. And he spoke to the wife in a soft voice. "Old woman, do you ever thank Almighty God for this man by your side?"

The old woman, though feeble of voice, did not hesitate for a second. "Indeed, indeed. After all the tribulations have been counted and weighed, they account for so much less than the days and nights of comfort. I have regrets in this life, but I do not regret that I bound up my life with this man's life."

Then the old man spoke. "Nor do I."

And at that the Traveler smiled, knowing that the words he read from The Book would not be wasted so long as this venerable pair and others like them lived to give the words meaning.

CHILDREN

WHILE the Unknown Traveler was speaking of marriage, the Valley's children played in the square, just as children have done for centuries upon centuries. The Traveler knew well the pain that children could bring to their families. Yet he also knew the incomparable delight a child's smile could bring to even the most jaded heart. He looked at a small boy—a wide-eyed boy with unruly hair—tugging anxiously on his father's sleeve, and then he spoke these words.

> Children are a gift from the Lord; they are a reward from him. Children born to a young man are like sharp arrows in a warrior's hands. How happy is the man whose quiver is full of them!

The Traveler could see the small boy had moved to the side of an older man, a man who placed a wrinkled but loving hand on the boy's head. He knew this was the child's grandfather, and he said this.

Grandchildren are the crowning glory of the aged; parents are the pride of their children.

Then the Traveler read this story of how the Son of God cared for little children.

One day some parents brought their children to Jesus so he could touch them and bless them, but the disciples told them not to bother him.

But when Jesus saw what was happening, he was very displeased with his disciples. He said to them, "Let the children come to me. Don't stop them! For the Kingdom of God belongs to such as these. I assure you, anyone who doesn't have their kind of faith will never get into the Kingdom of God."

Then he spoke these words, words he knew would chafe those who had no real love for life, born or unborn.

"Listen, People of the Valley. Life is a good gift from your Creator. Cherish life, guard it. Hear The Book's words about the beginning of life and children."

You made all the delicate, inner parts of my body and knit me together in my mother's womb. Thank you for making me so wonderfully complex! Your work-manship is marvelous—and how well I know it.

You watched me as I was being formed in utter seclusion, as I was woven together in the dark of the womb. You saw me before I was born. Every day of my life was recorded in your book. Every moment was laid out before a single day had passed.

The Traveler could see a small boy, a lonely, sullen boy, sitting on the ground, tracing meaningless patterns with a stick he was holding. The boy's father and mother were whispering to each other, clearly paying no heed to either the Traveler or their boy. The Traveler knew such parents well. He knew they were so occupied with their own affairs that they gave little thought or time to the child they had brought into the world. He knew that they would give the child little guidance as he matured. And they would cover up their own laziness and selfishness with empty words about how a child should be allowed to choose his own path and decide things for himself. And for them the Traveler read these words from The Book.

If you refuse to discipline your children, it proves you don't love them; if you love your children, you will be prompt to discipline them.

Discipline your children while there is hope. If you don't, you will ruin their lives.

A youngster's heart is filled with foolishness, but discipline will drive it away.

To discipline and reprimand a child produces wisdom, but a mother is disgraced by an undisciplined child.

Teach your children to choose the right path, and when they are older, they will remain upon it.

A wise child brings joy to a father; a foolish child brings grief to a mother.

On the other side of the square was a sad-faced girl, a girl whose pale eyes had been reddened with tears, not just today, but often. She, the Traveler could tell, was already full of anger and resentment. She did not lack for a mother's or father's discipline. What she lacked was a home where wisdom and self-control tempered strictness, adding love to the correcting hand. For the parents of such a child as this the Traveler lifted these words of The Book.

Don't make your children angry by the way you treat them. Rather, bring them up with the discipline and instruction approved by the Lord.

Amelia, a young woman whose face expressed a wisdom that many older people did not possess, stepped forward, all the while holding the hand of her young son.

"Sir," she said, "everything you say is true. But I have a friend whose daughter has broken her heart. She and her husband did what they could, and the other children turned out well. Yet one child did not. Are we alone responsible for what our children do? Have you nothing to say to the children themselves? Should they not have to bear some of the load?"

Her piercing eyes looked directly at the Traveler, and he knew this woman would not move until she had a reply. And he gave this answer from The Book—not to Amelia, and not to the other fathers and mothers, but to the children.

Children, obey your parents because you belong to the Lord, for this is the right thing to do. "Honor your father and mother." This is the first of the Ten Commandments that ends with a promise. And this is the promise: If you honor your father and mother, "you will live a long life, full of blessing.".

My son, obey your father's commands, and don't neglect your mother's teaching. Keep their words always in your heart. Tie them around your neck. Wherever you walk, their counsel can lead you. When you sleep, they will protect you. When you wake up in the morning, they will advise you. For these commands and this teaching are a lamp to light the way ahead of you. The correction of discipline is the way to life.

After reading this, the Unknown Traveler looked into Amelia's eyes and saw that she was satisfied with the answer.

"Young woman," he said, "love that child you are holding by the hand there. All of you fathers and mothers, listen. Be that beam of light spoken of in The Book. And you children, follow the light. No man, woman, or child can do anything better or wiser than this: Follow the light."

Perched on her father's shoulders, a little girl pulled playfully but gently at his beard, and his fingers intertwined with hers.

KNOWLEDGE

A MAN named Milo was a teacher, much loved by generations of students. For five decades Milo had taken the young ones of the Valley to a ridge and said to them, "All of this is yours, and greater things besides, if you have knowledge. You were born to know. This is what lifts you up from the mud and separates you from the beasts. There is nothing in this galaxy with its unnumbered stars that you cannot measure and count and dissect. And it may be someday that I will tell my students that the stars are, indeed, now numbered. This is your destiny. Know, analyze, control. Remind each other that the fences and the walls within your minds must be demolished. And if some part of the universe builds a wall around itself, shutting you out, tear down that wall."

Now Milo was in the square that day, listening to the Unknown Traveler, pleased to hear that someone was valiant for truth.

Milo spoke to the Traveler. "Sir, I have spent seventy years tracking down the truth, and fifty of those years guiding others toward it. Surely this Book, this treasure you have unearthed after all these centuries, will give us knowledge as we have never known."

"Knowledge indeed," said the Traveler, perceiving what sort of man he spoke to. "If knowledge had weight, you could not lift The Book. If it fell upon you, it would crush you like a boulder crushing a flea. And now I will read you The Book's first tale of knowledge. It concerns the first man and woman in the world. The loving Creator, having formed them from the dust and placed them in the loveliest of gardens, gave them all that could be desired. Yet they desired more. The fruit given them to eat was not enough. Like rebellious children, they ate from a tree called the Tree of Knowledge, a tree whose fruit the Lord had denied to them. And in doing this they changed forever that blessed state, the state of perfect harmony and perfect innocence, where they were naked and vulnerable yet not ashamed."

The serpent was the shrewdest of all the creatures the Lord God had made. "Really?" he asked the woman. "Did God really say you must not eat any of the fruit in the garden?"

"Of course we may eat it," the woman told him. "It's only the fruit from the tree at the center of the garden that we are not allowed to eat. God says we must not eat it or even touch it, or we will die."

"You won't die!" the serpent hissed. "God knows that your eyes will be opened when you eat it. You will become just like God, knowing everything, both good and evil."

The woman was convinced. The fruit looked so fresh and delicious, and it would make her so wise! So she ate some of the fruit. She also gave some to her husband, who was with her. Then he ate it, too. At that moment, their eyes were opened, and they suddenly felt shame at their nakedness. So they strung fig leaves together around their hips to cover themselves.

Toward evening they heard the Lord God walking about in the garden, so they hid themselves among the trees. The Lord God called to Adam, "Where are you?"

He replied, "I heard you, so I hid. I was afraid because I was naked."

"Who told you that you were naked?" the Lord God asked. "Have you eaten the fruit I commanded you not to eat?"

"Yes," Adam admitted, "but it was the woman you gave me who brought me the fruit, and I ate it."

And to Adam he said, "Because you listened to your wife and ate the fruit I told you not to eat, I have placed a curse on the ground. All your life you will struggle to scratch a living from it.

"All your life you will sweat to produce food, until your dying day. Then you will return to the ground from which you came. For you were made from dust, and to the dust you will return."

Milo blushed at this—not for himself, but for the Traveler. *How,* Milo said in his heart, *could this man stand before the people and read such mindless folk tales?*

Then Milo spoke aloud. "Do you want us to believe that we offend the God of heaven by seeking to be wise? I have taken a thousand students under my wing and shown them that God desires that we grow, learn, expand, grasp. And the God you speak of in your tale is not that same God. What sort of cruel Ruler would deny us what our minds can grasp?" And several of the People of the Valley who had loved Milo and gained from his instruction nodded in agreement. A few wandered back to their homes, full of the quiet indignity that some scholars wear so well. They were not inclined to bluster, for they believed only fools raved at other fools.

A young woman named Vivian had learned much

from Milo, and she came to his defense. "What our revered teacher says is true," she said with proper politeness, though the edges of her soft words had nettles. "Surely the One you say is the Source of Truth would not treat his creatures so."

The Traveler paused. This was not the first occasion when a listener had balked at the ageless story. "Were you not listening? The curse put upon man was not for seeking knowledge but for seeking to be like God. A creature— much loved, much gifted by his Maker, endowed with such faculties, blessed with the bounty of a world unspoiled— that creature wanted to be more than a creature. The man, made from the dust, wanted to forget his beginning."

The Traveler then sighed, seeing that even the wise disciples of Milo lacked so much understanding. "Beloved People of the Valley," he began, "surely you have seen that though you pile fact upon fact, making towers of them, making mountain ranges of them, you end by standing on them and seeing that there are cloud-shrouded mountains further in the distance. When you swallow a goblet full of knowledge, you then see that it came from a bottomless vat. Consider, then, these words from one of the wisest men who ever lifted up eye to consider this world."

I, the Teacher, was king of Israel, and I lived in Jerusalem. I devoted myself to search for understanding and to explore by wisdom everything being done in the world. I soon discovered that God has dealt a tragic existence to the human race.

I said to myself, "Look, I am wiser than any of the kings who ruled in Jerusalem before me. I have greater wisdom and knowledge than any of them." So I worked hard to distinguish wisdom from foolishness. But now I realize that even this was like chasing the wind. For the greater my wisdom, the greater my grief. To increase knowledge only increases sorrow.

Then the Unknown Traveler said, "The wise one, the king of Israel, had every pleasure open to him. And you learn from his words that pursuit of knowledge is no grander or nobler than the childish pursuit of pleasure. If you do not feel your vanities pricked by his confession, at least heed the words of the Lord himself."

Where were you when I laid the foundations of the earth? Tell me, if you know so much. Do you know how its dimensions were determined and who did the surveying? What supports its foundations, and who laid its cornerstone as the morning stars sang together and all the angels shouted for joy?

Who defined the boundaries of the sea as it burst from the womb, and as I clothed it with clouds and thick darkness? For I locked it behind barred gates, limiting its shores. I said, "Thus far and no farther will you come. Here your proud waves must stop!"

Have you ever commanded the morning to appear and caused the dawn to rise in the east? Have you ever told the daylight to spread to the ends of the earth, to bring an end to the night's wickedness? For the features of the earth take shape as the light approaches, and the dawn is robed in red. The light disturbs the haunts of the wicked, and it stops the arm that is raised in violence.

Have you explored the springs from which the seas come? Have you walked about and explored their depths? Do you know where the gates of death are located? Have you seen the gates of utter gloom? Do you realize the extent of the earth? Tell me about it if you know!

Where does the light come from, and where does the darkness go? Can you take it to its home? Do you know how to get there? But of course you know all this! For you were born before it was all created, and you are so very experienced!

Have you visited the treasuries of the snow? Have you seen where the hail is made and stored? I have reserved it for the time of trouble, for the day of battle and war. Where is the path to the origin of light? Where is the home of the east wind?

Who created a channel for the torrents of rain?

Who laid out the path for the lightning? Who makes the rain fall on barren land, in a desert where no one lives? Who sends the rain that satisfies the parched ground and makes the tender grass spring up?

Does the rain have a father? Where does dew come from? Who is the mother of the ice? Who gives birth to the frost from the heavens? For the water turns to ice as hard as rock, and the surface of the water freezes.

Can you hold back the movements of the stars? Are you able to restrain the Pleiades or Orion? Can you ensure the proper sequence of the seasons or guide the constellation of the Bear with her cubs across the heavens? Do you know the laws of the universe and how God rules the earth?

Can you shout to the clouds and make it rain? Can you make lightning appear and cause it to strike as you direct it? Who gives intuition and instinct? Who is wise enough to count all the clouds? Who can tilt the water jars of heaven, turning the dry dust to clumps of mud?

Then the Traveler said, "Even if you knew every corner of this boundless world, even if you had charted and mapped and recorded every line and point of it, what would you have done then? If you counted every grain of sand and numbered every feather on every bird that ever flew, would you be any more like the One who made the tides and sprinkled the skies with owls and falcons? Measurer is not Maker, and surveyor is not Sovereign. Yet how you delight in knowing, knowing, knowing, as though the substance there within your skulls had been placed there for nothing more than assuring itself that omniscience was within its reach."

Martin was listening to all this, remembering fondly how Milo had showed him the beating heart of an injured sparrow he nestled in his hand. And he and the other children had been delighted, running home to tell their parents what they had seen. Yet Martin had sat on the hillside only yesterday, a man perplexed and more than slightly hungry for the Truth. Now he believed that Milo, the wise and beloved Milo, had not pointed them toward truth—the Truth—but to will-of-the-wisps, to bubbles that now burst. And he swallowed, and down his throat went regret. It was not regret that he had learned so much about the world and its workings, but that the Framer of the world had not been studied or known or thanked for the variety and the order of his invention. And now he understood the story of the first man and woman, who chose to grasp for God's position and not to grasp for God himself.

Martin's youngest son was one of Milo's pupils. The son admired and respected his teacher, as Martin himself had done. The son, who was standing beside his father, looked into the weathered face of Milo, then spoke to the

Traveler. "Sir, we have been taught from the cradle that we were to learn all we could. Is it wrong to do so?"

The Traveler smiled. "Young one, learn all you can. But know that you cannot possibly learn everything. Some things are less worthy of your mind than others. And know that some are most worthy of all. The Great Being who made everything to be—surely he is most worthy of your attentions." And at that time Milo and the young woman Vivian left the square, talking to each other as they left. The Traveler watched them go, then read these words.

Anyone who claims to know all the answers doesn't really know very much. But the person who loves God is the one God knows and cares for.

Surely it is God's Spirit within people, the breath of the Almighty within them, that makes them intelligent. But sometimes the elders are not wise. Sometimes the aged do not understand justice.

Stop fooling yourselves. If you think you are wise by this world's standards, you will have to become a fool so you can become wise by God's standards. For the wisdom of this world is foolishness to God. As the Scriptures say,

"God catches those who think they are wise in their own cleverness."

No wonder people everywhere fear him. People who are truly wise show him reverence.

Destruction is certain for those who think they are wise and consider themselves to be clever.

"People of the Valley, loved by God, if anyone asked you to bring forth evidence of the wise ones' blessings to their fellow creatures, what would you bring? With all its delights, its tantalizing notions, its poetry, its ability to provoke both laughter and tears, knowledge by itself appears weak and unfulfilled. For since the world began spinning the philosophers and scholars are no more inclined than the village idiots to lift up the fallen and nurse the dying. When the helpless scream in desperation, the sages retreat as swiftly as the dunces. Love is as likely to set in kind motion the hands of an utter fool as the hands of the academy's master."

A small boy sat near the feet of his father, who was listening earnestly to the Traveler. The Traveler looked at the boy's wide, brown eyes and the pale, unlined forehead. And he said to the boy's father, "Pray every morning and every night, and at every hour throughout the day, that your son will love God so dearly that he will call him 'Father' as freely as he uses the word for you. Pray that even if this boy learns nothing else, that he will honor the one Being most deserving of honor." Then he read these words.

May you have the power to understand, as all God's people should, how wide, how long, how high, and how deep his love really is. May you experience the love of Christ, though it is so great you will never fully understand it. Then you will be filled with the fullness of life and power that comes from God.

Oh, what a wonderful God we have! How great are his riches and wisdom and knowledge! How impossible it is for us to understand his decisions and his methods! For who can know what the Lord is thinking? Who knows enough to be his counselor? And who could ever give him so much that he would have to pay it back?

For everything comes from him; everything exists by his power and is intended for his glory. To him be glory evermore.

When he had read those words, a young woman whose limbs sometimes shook uncontrollably and whose head constantly nodded said in a loud voice, "Glory evermore!"

Martin's son tugged on his father's sleeve and said, "That's the feeble-minded girl who cannot read. And she still plays with dolls."

And Martin said to his son, "If those of us whose minds are whole and vigorous do not praise God joyfully, then it is we who are feeble-minded." Then the two of them heard a simple-hearted giggle from the girl, and Martin wondered if it was her way of praising the Creator.

the
self

A YOUNG woman named Candice lived in the Valley, as did her mother, and the two loved each other much and quarreled much. And she saw, as every grown child does, her mother's imperfections clearly. At times Candice loved her mother without questioning. And at times she would blame the ills of the world on her mother's failings.

The Unknown Traveler knew that such things occurred in the Valley, for they occurred everywhere. Children were wise enough to see their father's and mother's errors, yet cheerfully blind to their own. If a flood came in the child's life, it was because the parent had summoned up the clouds.

But the Traveler also knew how parents sometimes caused, though without intention, their children to become vain and self-absorbed. And they did so in the name of love, a name used to cover up much of the world's folly. So for generation after generation parent and child never so fully unite as in this one endeavor, the creation of perplexed and thoughtless children, children who learn only with difficulty that they are not the axis of the universe.

Candice, who was regarded by her friends as lacking in confidence, often complained of the lack of encouragement her mother had given her. She was certain that other children had received their fair share, while she had not. She believed this had engendered a lack of respect for herself. And since her mother was standing near her, and since the Traveler was there in the square to lead the people to the Truth, Candice believed that he would serve to then and there convict her mother of her defects.

"Sir," she said, "you tell us that our love for God is a sublime thing. But is it not right to love ourselves? We have all known the agony of hating ourselves, believing we were of no value, believing our few virtues paled next to our shortcomings, believing our minds and passions had no capacity for greatness. If some of this world's ills are due to our treason in not saluting the Governor of the cosmos, then surely some are due to that disabling treason of despising ourselves."

Many of Candice's friends nodded. And even a few parents nodded, for some willingly accepted guilt for their children's lack of self-love.

The Traveler held up The Book and said calmly, "Here are the words. Surely you all remember them. Humankind was made in the image of God, upright, and pure. Your first parents tried to be like God, and ever afterward the harmony they first possessed has eluded you. Yet the sacred image in you is not erased, blurred though it is." Then the Traveler began to read.

O Lord, our Lord, the majesty of your name fills the earth! Your glory is higher than the heavens.

When I look at the night sky and see the work of your fingers—the moon and the stars you have set in place—what are mortals that you should think of us, mere humans that you should care for us?

For you made us only a little lower than God, and you crowned us with glory and honor. You put us in charge of everything you made, giving us authority over all things—the sheep and the cattle and all the wild animals, the birds in the sky, the fish in the sea, and everything that swims the ocean currents.

"Do these words lift this burden you claim to have? This weight of self-loathing you claim to sweat beneath—is it dispelled by hearing that the Lord God still gives man, sinful though he is, dominion over this world? Is this all you wished to hear, or would you like to hear more of the Truth?" Then he read again.

"The human heart is most deceitful and desperately wicked. Who really knows how bad it is? But I know! I, the Lord, search all hearts and examine secret motives."

The Lord looks down from heaven on the entire human race; he looks to see if there is even one with real understanding, one who seeks for God. But no, all have turned away from God; all have become corrupt. No one does good, not even one!

Claiming to be wise, they became utter fools instead. And instead of worshiping the glorious, ever-living God, they worshiped idols made to look like mere people, or birds and animals and snakes.

When they refused to acknowledge God, he abandoned them to their evil minds and let them do things that should never be done. Their lives became full of every kind of wickedness, sin, greed, hate, envy, murder, fighting, deception, malicious behavior, and gossip.

These wicked people are too proud to seek God. They seem to think that God is dead.

They say to themselves, "Nothing bad will ever happen to us! We will be free of trouble forever!"

Their mouths are full of cursing, lies, and threats. Trouble and evil are on the tips of their tongues. They lurk in dark alleys, murdering the innocent who pass by. They are always searching for some helpless

victim. Like lions they crouch silently, waiting to
pounce on the helpless. Like hunters they capture
their victims and drag them away in nets. The helpless
are overwhelmed and collapse; they fall beneath the
strength of the wicked. The wicked say to themselves,
"God isn't watching! He will never notice!"

Only fools say in their hearts, "There is no God."

A certain bright-eyed young man, a friend of Candice,
said to the Traveler, "Sir, you speak to us of extremes. There
are indeed wicked people walking the globe. But most of us
here are reasonable folk, pleased to work for our livings, visit
those we love, rear our children, and harm no one. We tend
our own gardens. And if we wake at night, feeling a vague
pain gnawing in us, it is not guilt over our crimes. It is
contempt for ourselves. And why that contempt is in us we
cannot explain. But we know it is wrong."

"Are you so certain? How do you think you appear to
the Creator when you come before him, honoring yourselves?" Then the Traveler read them this story told by the
Son of God.

Two men went to the Temple to pray. One was a
Pharisee, and the other was a dishonest tax collector.
The proud Pharisee stood by himself and prayed this
prayer: "I thank you, God, that I am not a sinner like
everyone else, especially like that tax collector over

there! For I never cheat, I don't sin, I don't commit adultery, I fast twice a week, and I give you a tenth of my income."

But the tax collector stood at a distance and dared not even lift his eyes to heaven as he prayed. Instead, he beat his chest in sorrow, saying, "O God, be merciful to me, for I am a sinner."

I tell you, this sinner, not the Pharisee, returned home justified before God. For the proud will be humbled, but the humble will be honored.

"Dear People of the Valley, though you were made in the image of God, you are a fallen, marred race. Do you understand this? Inside you mingle angel and beast together, and the two are at war in even those who appear principled. And even when you have cast out the grosser sins from your lives—murder, theft, and all that are easily visible to observers—then you are still clinging to the pet sin, the sin of the righteous, which is pride. And yet you come to me, wanting me to read you words affirming your pride and self-love.

"I cannot read such affirmations from The Book, for they are not there. These pages will not encourage your self-lauding. For the God of heaven knows your hearts, and he knows that no man or woman will find joy in being 'I' unless there is a 'they' to look down upon. A person by himself or a group banding together—when human beings begin to applaud their own goodness and their own uniqueness, then they begin to hiss someone else's loathsomeness. There is no pride without prejudice. When you announce to the world 'I am good' or 'We are good,' you announce your contempt for someone else. You wish this was not so, but it is so. Do not think you can cast out your self-hate and fill up the void with self-love. You are impotent in this."

The Traveler could in some eyes see a hint of gloom, and in some there was the low fire of indignation. He knew these words were of no comfort, and he did not wish to leave the people empty. So he said, "The Book will not give you what you asked for—not in regard to your pride. But I will read something else to you." And he said to them these words from the Son of God.

> If you are invited to a wedding feast, don't always head for the best seat. What if someone more respected than you has also been invited?
>
> Do this instead—sit at the foot of the table. Then when your host sees you, he will come and say, "Friend, we have a better place than this for you!" Then you will be honored in front of all the other guests. For the proud will be humbled, but the humble will be honored.
>
> The greatest among you must be a servant. But those who exalt themselves will be humbled, and those who humble themselves will be exalted.

Then the bright-eyed young man said to the Traveler, "Is this the cure for all our discomfort? If we act humbly, have we fulfilled our duty to God and quieted our insides?" And he asked this with hesitation, for he was still unsure of the rightness of humility.

The Traveler shook his head. "Humility is in human eyes a muddy stone, but a polished diamond in the eyes of God. Yet how perverse your hearts are—you who ask me to sanction your love of self. There are humble men and women who lock their doors at night, kneeling before the Almighty, so proud of their humility that it hangs like a thick veil between them and the Captain of earth and heaven. Pride prevents the discernment of pride. You cannot see your own eyes because you are inside them, looking outward. So it is with pride. It hides itself well. And so do a thousand other petty sins."

Then the Traveler read these words of a sinful man who begged to be given clear eyes.

How can I know all the sins lurking in my heart? Cleanse me from these hidden faults. Keep me from deliberate sins! Don't let them control me. Then I will be free of guilt and innocent of great sin.

"How are we to be cleansed?" asked Candice. "You have made it clear to us that we are powerless to help ourselves. You preach to us a philosophy of dismay."

"That is what it is," said the Traveler. "That is the purpose of The Book. It will lead you to despair. You want me to tell you you are good. I tell you instead that you are fallen, marred. I tell you that your own attempts to press the seal of validity on your existence will come to nothing. I tell you that your restlessness comes not from lack of self-love, but from lack of reality. For until you face yourselves in clear mirrors and acknowledge your fallenness, you will have sleepless nights. Consider the words of one of the holy ones, a man on fire for God. Hear his confession of his weakness."

I don't understand myself at all, for I really want to do what is right, but I don't do it. Instead, I do the very thing I hate. I know perfectly well that what I am doing is wrong, and my bad conscience shows that I agree that the law is good. But I can't help myself, because it is sin inside me that makes me do these evil things.

I know I am rotten through and through so far as my old sinful nature is concerned. No matter which way I turn, I can't make myself do right. I want to, but I can't. When I want to do good, I don't. And when I try not to do wrong, I do it anyway. But if I am doing what I don't want to do, I am not really the one doing it; the sin within me is doing it.

It seems to be a fact of life that when I want to do what is right, I inevitably do what is wrong. I love

God's law with all my heart. But there is another law at work within me that is at war with my mind. This law wins the fight and makes me a slave to the sin that is still within me. Oh, what a miserable person I am! Who will free me from this life that is dominated by sin?

Thank God! The answer is in Jesus Christ our Lord. So you see how it is: In my mind I really want to obey God's law, but because of my sinful nature I am a slave to sin.

"Do you hear in these words despair? But The Book was not meant to leave you in despair. It was written to tell you that the means to destroy your pride is to dwell on the greatness of God and his Son."

No one can ever boast in the presence of God.

Be honest in your estimate of yourselves, measuring your value by how much faith God has given you.

Be sure to do what you should, for then you will enjoy the personal satisfaction of having done your work well, and you won't need to compare yourself to anyone else. For we are each responsible for our own conduct.

"The Book will not stoke your dreams of elevating yourselves. This is not a book of phantoms, but The Book of

God. And it says to you, 'Reality above all else,' for it comes from the Great Reality who formed it all. And embracing reality, you will see your own failures. And if you lift up your eyes to look beyond them, you will see the grandeur and the mercy of the Holy One. For he says to the fallen and the failing that they are most acceptable when they own up to their deeds and misdeeds. He says to those who bewail their limitations, 'You do not have to be me. Your role as a limited, finite being is acceptable to me.' This begins as the philosophy of dismay, but it becomes the philosophy of triumph."

Then he read to them the words of a finite, failing man who had stepped beyond despair by looking at God.

> O Lord, you have examined my heart and know everything about me. You know when I sit down or stand up. You know my every thought when far away. You chart the path ahead of me and tell me where to stop and rest.
>
> Every moment you know where I am. You know what I am going to say even before I say it, Lord. you both precede and follow me. you place your hand of blessing on my head.
>
> Such knowledge is too wonderful for me, too great for me to know! I can never escape from your spirit! I can never get away from your presence! If I go up to heaven, you are there; if I go down to the place of the dead, you are there.

How precious are your thoughts about me,
O God! They are innumerable! I can't even count
them; they outnumber the grains of sand! And when
I wake up in the morning, you are still with me!

Search me, O God, and know my heart; test me
and know my thoughts. Point out anything in me
that offends you, and lead me along the path of
everlasting life.

And there was nothing else to be said about the self.
Though Candice and her friends were bewildered and
annoyed by the Traveler's words, some of the People of the
Valley took comfort, knowing they did not have to exhaust
the costly energy of life in building themselves up. Martin,
who had been young once, believed now that God was best
at being God. In the blood of this finite man surged not
self-loathing, but joy. And Martin said to himself, *Better to
be accepted and embraced by the Divine One than to strive at
being divine.*

MONEY AND POSSESSIONS

NEAR THE square stood the home of a rich trader named Vincent. He had not joined the people gathered in the square because he could observe everything clearly from his balcony.

As Vincent surveyed the scene, he saw all sorts of people. Some of his friends, other rich men, were there. And there were those who had practically no possessions to speak of. Vincent looked down and wondered if this loving Father written about in The Book had indeed made both the rich man and the poor man.

Vincent saw Martin, with whom he had done business in years past. Martin was neither rich nor poor, yet like many of the People of the Valley, Martin had worked hard much of his life. Vincent said to himself, *Did the same*

God who made me make Martin—and that penniless drifter
there on the other side of the square? Or does this God even
take notice of who possesses what?

In a pleasant, businesslike voice, Vincent called
down from his balcony to the Unknown Traveler. "You
there—what does The Book say about money and homes
and clothing and such?" Since Vincent was polite and a
proper businessman, he did not wish to sound too inquisi-
tive. But his question was sincere nonetheless.

The Traveler looked toward the man on the balcony.
He could see the silk and the gold that Vincent had draped
himself with. And he began to read from The Book.

> The rich think of their wealth as an impregnable
> defense; they imagine it is a high wall of safety.
>
> Rich people picture themselves as wise, but their
> real poverty is evident to the poor.
>
> Like a bird that hatches eggs she has not laid, so
> are those who get their wealth by unjust means.
> Sooner or later they will lose their riches and, at the
> end of their lives, will become poor old fools.
>
> Jesus said to his disciples, "I tell you the truth, it is
> very hard for a rich person to get into the Kingdom
> of Heaven. I say it again—it is easier for a camel to
> go through the eye of a needle than for a rich person
> to enter the Kingdom of God!
>
> "No one can serve two masters. For you will hate

one and love the other, or be devoted to one and despise the other. You cannot serve both God and money."

Vincent appeared not to be bothered by these words. He absentmindedly ran his forefinger across the lavender silk shirt he wore. The Traveler continued reading.

A rich man had a fertile farm that produced fine crops. In fact, his barns were full to overflowing. So he said, "I know! I'll tear down my barns and build bigger ones. Then I'll have room enough to store everything. And I'll sit back and say to myself, My friend, you have enough stored away for years to come. Now take it easy! Eat, drink, and be merry!"

But God said to him, "You fool! You will die this very night. Then who will get it all?"

Yes, a person is a fool to store up earthly wealth but not have a rich relationship with God.

This was not the first time Vincent had heard someone speak this way about wealth. But he knew that most people lived and moved in the realm of envy. So when he heard people speak against wealth, he perceived that they only wanted what he had. Now, listening to the words the Traveler read, he was perplexed, for he realized that the

God who made the world and everything in it could not envy a rich man. So he spoke again to the Traveler.

"Say more about this, Traveler. Tell us more about God and why he denies the rich what they have."

The Traveler began to read again from The Book.

Look here, you rich people, weep and groan with anguish because of all the terrible troubles ahead of you. Your wealth is rotting away, and your fine clothes are moth-eaten rags. Your gold and silver have become worthless. The very wealth you were counting on will eat away your flesh in hell. This treasure you have accumulated will stand as evidence against you on the day of judgment.

For listen! Hear the cries of the field workers whom you have cheated of their pay. The wages you held back cry out against you. The cries of the reapers have reached the ears of the Lord Almighty.

You have spent your years on earth in luxury, satisfying your every whim. Now your hearts are nice and fat, ready for the slaughter. You have condemned and killed good people who had no power to defend themselves against you.

Then Vincent withdrew into his house, not wanting to hear more.

The Traveler knew that the People of the Valley

envied Vincent and others like him. When Vincent left
the balcony, a vagrant, whose home was the square because
he had no other home, watched the elegant curtains on
the balcony as they rustled sleepily in the autumn breeze.
And for such men as this penniless one the Unknown
Traveler read these words from The Book.

> Don't be dismayed when the wicked grow rich, and
> their homes become ever more splendid. For when
> they die, they carry nothing with them. Their wealth
> will not follow them into the grave. In this life they
> consider themselves fortunate, and the world loudly
> applauds their success. But they will die like all others
> before them and never again see the light of day.
>
> They seem to live such a painless life; their bodies
> are so healthy and strong. They aren't troubled like
> other people or plagued with problems like everyone
> else. They wear pride like a jeweled necklace, and
> their clothing is woven of cruelty. These fat cats
> have everything their hearts could ever wish for!
> They scoff and speak only evil; in their pride they
> seek to crush others. They boast against the very
> heavens, and their words strut throughout the earth.
>
> And so the people are dismayed and confused,
> drinking in all their words. "Does God realize what is
> going on?" they ask. "Is the Most High even aware of

what is happening?" Look at these arrogant people—
enjoying a life of ease while their riches multiply.

The vagrants in the town square heard these questions from The Book, and they recognized them as questions their own hearts had uttered.

I tried to understand why the wicked prosper. But
what a difficult task it is! Then one day I went into
your sanctuary, O God, and I thought about the
destiny of the wicked. Truly, you put them on a slip-
pery path and send them sliding over the cliff to
destruction. In an instant they are destroyed, swept
away by terrors. Their present life is only a dream
that is gone when they awake. When you arise,
O Lord, you will make them vanish from this life.

Beware! Don't be greedy for what you don't have.
Real life is not measured by how much we own.

It is better to be godly and have little than to be
evil and possess much.

It is better to have little with fear for the Lord
than to have great treasure with turmoil.

It is better to be poor and godly than rich and
dishonest.

Don't weary yourself trying to get rich. Why waste
your time? For riches can disappear as though they
had the wings of a bird!

The Traveler said to the People of the Valley,
"There are wells reputed to be bottomless. It is said that
you could pour into them forever and ever and they would
not be filled. But no one has tried this. But some have tried
to fill themselves, and they have failed." And he began to
read again.

Those who love money will never have enough. How
absurd to think that wealth brings true happiness!
The more you have, the more people come to help
you spend it. So what is the advantage of wealth—
except perhaps to watch it run through your fingers!

People who work hard sleep well, whether they
eat little or much. But the rich are always worrying
and seldom get a good night's sleep.

Yet true religion with contentment is great
wealth. After all, we didn't bring anything with us
when we came into the world, and we certainly
cannot carry anything with us when we die. So if we
have enough food and clothing, let us be content.
But people who long to be rich fall into temptation
and are trapped by many foolish and harmful desires
that plunge them into ruin and destruction. For the
love of money is at the root of all kinds of evil. And
some people, craving money, have wandered from
the faith and pierced themselves with many sorrows.

Vincent's butler stood on the balcony. He was troubled at these words, for he loved the family he had served for three decades. Yet he also knew that they loved their wealth. And he felt led to speak in their defense, though he could not express himself with much conviction. He said in a placid voice to the Traveler, "Your words are harsh, Traveler."

"They are not my words," the Traveler said. "They are the words of The Book, and The Book is true, though the truth bites. I would be cruel, and The Book would not be true, if it only whispered and nuzzled." Then he read these words.

They trust in their wealth and boast of great riches. Yet they cannot redeem themselves from death by paying a ransom to God. Redemption does not come so easily, for no one can ever pay enough to live forever and never see the grave.

Those who are wise must finally die, just like the foolish and senseless, leaving all their wealth behind. The grave is their eternal home, where they will stay forever. They may name their estates after themselves, but they leave their wealth to others. They will not last long despite their riches—they will die like the animals.

This is the fate of fools, though they will be remembered as being so wise. Like sheep, they are led to the grave, where death will be their shepherd. In the morning the godly will rule over them. Their bodies will rot in the grave, far from their grand estates.

Vincent then appeared on his balcony again. He had been listening to the Traveler inside his house. Then he spoke again, barely controlling the anger welling up inside him.

"Sir, we live in a world of foolishness and contradictions. We are told from the cradle on that it is a grand thing to prosper and have much to show for it. Then we are told to despise what we have, or to feel the pains of guilt. Who can do right in such a world?"

"Were you not listening?" the Traveler asked him. "I read to you the words about a man serving two masters. What is it that you worship? Worship is what matters. If you feel guilt biting at your insides, let it not be guilt over your house or your clothing or the number of employees you have. Let it be guilt over gaining by burdening and defrauding others. But even if you have come by all your wealth honestly, do not rest too easily. You may feel guilt, and if so, let it be guilt over the devotion you gave to that frigid idol, money." He paused, and Vincent waited anxiously for his next words. "A rich man can be saved. It is hard, but not impossible. It is not *having*, but *worshiping* money that keeps rich men from the kingdom of God."

Then the Traveler began to read again, and his words were for both the rich and the poor.

The rich and the poor have this in common: The Lord made them both.

The poor and the oppressor have this in common—the Lord gives light to the eyes of both.

The Lord makes one poor and another rich; he brings one down and lifts another up. He lifts the poor from the dust—yes, from a pile of ashes! He treats them like princes, placing them in seats of honor. For all the earth is the Lord's, and he has set the world in order.

Give me neither poverty nor riches! Give me just enough to satisfy my needs. For if I grow rich, I may deny you and say, "Who is the Lord?" and if I am too poor, I may steal and thus insult God's holy name.

Christians who are poor should be glad, for God has honored them. And those who are rich should be glad, for God has humbled them. They will fade away like a flower in the field. The hot sun rises and dries up the grass; the flower withers, and its beauty fades away. So also, wealthy people will fade away with all of their achievements.

But because I have done what is right, I will see you. When I awake, I will be fully satisfied, for I will see you face to face.

Seeing the haggard and fretful face of the man who slept in the town square and owned nothing, the Traveler read these words, words from the mouth of the Son of God himself.

Don't worry about everyday life—whether you have enough food, drink, and clothes. Doesn't life consist of more than food and clothing? Look at the birds. They don't need to plant or harvest or put food in barns because your heavenly Father feeds them. And you are far more valuable to him than they are. Can all your worries add a single moment to your life? Of course not.

"And why worry about your clothes? Look at the lilies and how they grow. They don't work or make their clothing, yet Solomon in all his glory was not dressed as beautifully as they are. And if God cares so wonderfully for flowers that are here today and gone tomorrow, won't he more surely care for you? You have so little faith!

So don't worry about having enough food or drink or clothing. Why be like the pagans who are so deeply concerned about these things? Your heavenly Father already knows all your needs, and he will give you all you need from day to day if you live for him and make the Kingdom of God your primary concern.

So don't worry about tomorrow, for tomorrow will bring its own worries. Today's trouble is enough for today.

He read these words because he knew that frail humans often despair in a world where injustice seems to swallow up justice, a world where a small worry can gnaw away the foundations of the surest confidence. Then to strengthen what little faith they had, he read these words.

This is what the Lord says: "Let not the wise man gloat in his wisdom, or the mighty man in his might, or the rich man in his riches.

"Let them boast in this alone: that they truly know me and understand that I am the Lord who is just and righteous, whose love is unfailing, and that I delight in these things. I, the Lord, have spoken!"

"People, know that tonight you sit at your dinner under the eye of the One who knit together every child ever born, whether he was birthed on a bed of silk or in a cattle stall. And if you feast on basted pheasant or on the crumbs that the stray dogs bypass, you and what you eat and what you wear belong to that One." And some wondered if, in God's Kingdom, rich and poor would indeed sit at table together.

GIVING

THE PEOPLE of the Valley were intrigued by what the Unknown Traveler read to them about money and possessions. Like men and women of every age and every place, they would often neglect matters invisible to their eyes, but they could not forget about the firm material world and the share of it they possessed or wished to possess. The Traveler knew this, and he did not mind, for he knew that God himself had made the material world and took much pleasure in it.

A man named Giles had kinsmen in the Valley, and these were much poorer than he. As he lay in a comfortable bed at night, Giles often wondered if his relations were as comfortable as he was. Yet thoughts of them would vanish like a vapor when Giles told himself, *They deserve what they have, just as I do. It is not my concern.* Yet the thoughts would come back again, like an animal scratching at the door, begging to be let in.

Giles remembered these night thoughts as he stood in the square, watching the russet leaves of the autumn oaks rustling. *It is late in the year,* he said to himself, and somehow the waning of the season made him wish to speak to the Traveler.

"Sir, tell us about giving."

The Traveler looked at Giles and noticed that he resembled another man standing in the square. He could tell these were kin, though except for their faces there was nothing in common between them. Their clothes and their cleanness were nothing alike. Then the Traveler said, "I cannot speak about giving without speaking about the poor and the helpless. You live in a world of vanity and selfishness, and in such a world the ones in need are those who have no power, no influence, no voice. The penniless man, the woman born with no limbs, the child with an afflicted mind, the baby denied birth, the old couple abandoned by their family—these are the ones you must think of when you think of giving." Then he began to read.

Blessed are those who are generous, because they feed the poor.

Whoever gives to the poor will lack nothing. But

a curse will come upon those who close their eyes to poverty.

Oh, the joys of those who are kind to the poor. The Lord rescues them in times of trouble.

It is sin to despise one's neighbors; blessed are those who help the poor.

If you help the poor, you are lending to the Lord—and he will repay you!

Always judge your neighbors fairly, neither favoring the poor nor showing deference to the rich.

Give fair judgment to the poor and the orphan; uphold the rights of the oppressed and the destitute. Rescue the poor and helpless; deliver them from the grasp of evil people.

Tell those who are rich in this world not to be proud and not to trust in their money, which will soon be gone. But their trust should be in the living God, who richly gives us all we need for our enjoyment. Tell them to use their money to do good. They should be rich in good works and should give generously to those in need, always being ready to share with others whatever God has given them. By doing this they will be storing up their treasure as a good foundation for the future so that they may take hold of real life.

The godly know the rights of the poor; the wicked don't care to know.

The kind of fasting I want calls you to free those

who are wrongly imprisoned and to stop oppressing
those who work for you. Treat them fairly and give
them what they earn. I want you to share your food
with the hungry and to welcome poor wanderers into
your homes. Give clothes to those who need them,
and do not hide from relatives who need your help.

Give to those who ask, and don't turn away from
those who want to borrow.

Don't forget about those in prison. Suffer with
them as though you were there yourself. Share the
sorrow of those being mistreated, as though you feel
their pain in your own bodies.

And if you give even a cup of cold water to one of
the least of my followers, you will surely be rewarded.

If you do these things, your salvation will come
like the dawn. Yes, your healing will come quickly.
Your godliness will lead you forward, and the glory of
the Lord will protect you from behind.

Martin was listening closely. He believed these words
were directed to the rich people there. Yet he knew he
himself had enough to share at least something with those
who had less. So now he addressed the Traveler. "Sir, can
you give us rules or guidelines for giving?"

The Traveler looked with compassion on this man,
the first of the Valley's inhabitants he had encountered.
He understood Martin's heart, though he had met him

only that day. He knew Martin was a comfortable man, yet an uncomfortable man, a man with questions, a searching man. And he knew that searching people often feel desperate, and that desperation yearns for quick solutions and tidy formulas. So the Traveler asked him, "Do you know the meaning of 'tithe,' Martin?"

Martin replied, "It means a tenth part—ten percent. Is that what we are required to give?"

The Traveler understood clearly how such words as *require* and *percentage* could well mean the end of genuine giving and compassion. So he read to the people these words.

On every Lord's Day, each of you should put aside some amount of money in relation to what you have earned and save it for this offering.

If you are really eager to give, it isn't important how much you are able to give. God wants you to give what you have, not what you don't have.

Remember this—a farmer who plants only a few seeds will get a small crop. But the one who plants generously will get a generous crop. You must each make up your own mind as to how much you should give. Don't give reluctantly or in response to pressure. For God loves the person who gives cheerfully. And God will generously provide all you need. Then you will always have everything you need and plenty left over to share with others. As the Scriptures say,

"Godly people give generously to the poor.

Their good deeds will never be forgotten."

If you give, you will receive. Your gift will return to you in full measure, pressed down, shaken together to make room for more, and running over. Whatever measure you use in giving—large or small—it will be used to measure what is given back to you.

When he had read these words, the Traveler said, "Did you not know that any act of kindness you do is done for the Son of God himself?"

A young woman asked, "How can that be? We know that the Son of God once walked the earth as a man of flesh and blood. But he is not here now."

Pleased at the woman's attentiveness, the Traveler then read this parable told by the Son of God, who was speaking of the judgment that would take place at the end of the world.

When the Son of Man comes in his glory, and all the angels with him, then he will sit upon his glorious throne. All the nations will be gathered in his presence, and he will separate them as a shepherd separates the sheep from the goats. He will place the sheep at his right hand and the goats at his left.

Then the King will say to those on the right, "Come, you who are blessed by my Father, inherit the Kingdom prepared for you from the foundation of the world. For I was hungry, and you fed me. I was thirsty, and you gave me a drink. I was a stranger, and you invited me into your home. I was naked, and you gave me clothing. I was sick, and you cared for me. I was in prison, and you visited me."

Then these righteous ones will reply, "Lord, when did we ever see you hungry and feed you? Or thirsty and give you something to drink? Or a stranger and show you hospitality? Or naked and give you clothing? When did we ever see you sick or in prison, and visit you?" And the King will tell them, "I assure you, when you did it to one of the least of these my brothers and sisters, you were doing it to me!"

Then the King will turn to those on the left and say, "Away with you, you cursed ones, into the eternal fire prepared for the Devil and his demons! For I was hungry, and you didn't feed me. I was thirsty, and you didn't give me anything to drink. I was a stranger, and you didn't invite me into your home. I was naked, and you gave me no clothing. I was sick and in prison, and you didn't visit me."

Then they will reply, "Lord, when did we ever see you hungry or thirsty or a stranger or naked or sick or in prison, and not help you?" And he will answer, "I assure you, when you refused to help the least of these my brothers and sisters, you were refusing to help me."

A woman named Lila was considered by her friends to be a devout woman, a woman who understood the things of the soul. She asked the Traveler, "Sir, is it not true that God cares more for our spiritual needs than our material needs? Should we not seek more for what is eternal than for what passes away?"

These words were not new to the ears of the Traveler. While walking the roads of a selfish world he had seen that men and women often cover up their callousness with eloquent excuses. For such as these the Traveler read these words from The Book.

Suppose you see a brother or sister who needs food or clothing, and you say, "Well, good-bye and God bless you; stay warm and eat well"—but then you don't give that person any food or clothing. What good does that do?

If anyone has enough money to live well and sees a brother or sister in need and refuses to help—how can God's love be in that person?

Dear children, let us stop just saying we love each other; let us really show it by our actions. It is by our actions that we know we are living in the truth, so we will be confident when we stand before the Lord.

A very wealthy man was there, and his face beamed as he listened to these words. While the Traveler was reading, this man glanced around him and noticed some people looking at him with approval. And he was pleased, for he had given freely to charities of various kinds. He was regarded by all who knew him as a magnanimous giver, though he was often bothered by the Valley's vagrants passing through his property. He cleared his throat and said to the Traveler, "Well spoken, every word of it. What you have said I say to all my friends. We who have much must give much."

The Traveler could discern the man's assurance and self-satisfaction. He began to read again from The Book.

> Take care! Don't do your good deeds publicly, to be admired, because then you will lose the reward from your Father in heaven.
>
> When you give a gift to someone in need, don't shout about it as the hypocrites do—blowing trumpets in the synagogues and streets to call attention to their acts of charity! I assure you, they have received all the reward they will ever get.
>
> But when you give to someone, don't tell your left hand what your right hand is doing. Give your gifts in secret, and your Father, who knows all secrets, will reward you.

When the Traveler spoke these words, the wealthy man withdrew from the square. He was a busy man, and he had heard enough for one day.

Martin saw him walking away, and he said to the Traveler, "What you have read makes sense. You are saying that motivation is what matters. What is righteous is not the deed of kindness itself, but the chaste heart from which the deed issues."

The Traveler nodded in approval, then read them this story of the Son of God's meeting with a man whose heart became chaste.

Jesus entered Jericho and made his way through the town. There was a man there named Zacchaeus. He was one of the most influential Jews in the Roman tax-collecting business, and he had become very rich. He tried to get a look at Jesus, but he was too short to see over the crowds. So he ran ahead and climbed a sycamore tree beside the road, so he could watch from there.

When Jesus came by, he looked up at Zacchaeus and called him by name. "Zacchaeus!" he said. "Quick, come down! For I must be a guest in your home today."

Zacchaeus quickly climbed down and took Jesus to his house in great excitement and joy. But the crowds were displeased. "He has gone to be the guest of a notorious sinner," they grumbled.

Meanwhile, Zacchaeus stood there and said to the Lord, "I will give half my wealth to the poor, Lord, and if I have overcharged people on their taxes, I will give them back four times as much!"

Jesus responded, "Salvation has come to this home today, for this man has shown himself to be a son of Abraham. And I, the Son of Man, have come to seek and save those like him who are lost."

And when Martin heard this, he smiled, and it was the smile of one whose heart and mind had been stretched by the Truth. The Unknown Traveler was pleased to see his joy, for it was for this that he had come to the Valley.

WORK
AND
PLAY

A MAN with callused hands stood among the people. His name was Marcus, and he had toiled many years. His father and his father's father had taught him that work was the chief end of life. And he had believed this, though his heart often filled up with bitterness, angry that his days had seemed nothing more than a mingling of sweat and weariness and small gains.

Marcus could see among the people the man he had labored under for many years. When he looked at this man's fair skin, the fine texture of his hands, and the neatness of his clothes, Marcus clenched his fists. Then he thought of his father and his words about the dignity of labor. And he wondered if the Traveler had anything to tell the people about work.

Marcus's employer, who always spoke with measured dignity, addressed the Traveler, hoping the Traveler would speak words to encourage the workers' diligence.

"Sir, does The Book have anything to tell these people about the value of hard work?"

The Unknown Traveler understood this man and his purpose, yet he spoke these words from The Book, words which at first satisfied the employer.

Hard work means prosperity; only fools idle away their time.

Work hard and become a leader; be lazy and become a slave.

Lazy people don't even cook the game they catch, but the diligent make use of everything they find.

Lazy people want much but get little, but those who work hard will prosper and be satisfied.

An empty stable stays clean, but no income comes from an empty stable.

The Traveler was holding The Book high. Then he began to speak again, knowing that Marcus and people like him were present.

"Does it pain some of you to lift up your heads to see this? Are some of you so weary from your labor that your backs and necks are bent? Listen to the words of one who questioned the value of work."

I even found great pleasure in hard work, an additional reward for all my labors. But as I looked at everything I had worked so hard to accomplish, it was all so meaningless. It was like chasing the wind. There was nothing really worthwhile anywhere.

I am disgusted that I must leave the fruits of my hard work to others. And who can tell whether my successors will be wise or foolish? And yet they will control everything I have gained by my skill and hard work. How meaningless!

So I turned in despair from hard work. It was not the answer to my search for satisfaction in this life. For though I do my work with wisdom, knowledge, and skill, I must leave everything I gain to people who haven't worked to earn it. This is not only foolish but highly unfair.

So what do people get for all their hard work? Their days of labor are filled with pain and grief; even at night they cannot rest. It is all utterly meaningless.

How frail is humanity! How short is life, and how full of trouble! Like a flower, we blossom for a moment and then wither. Like the shadow of a passing cloud, we quickly disappear.

"True, true!" It was Marcus who spoke, and words did not come easily to Marcus. "So what is the point of it all, then? We break our backs, and someone else benefits."

The Traveler had compassion on this man. He smiled the smile of understanding and pity, and Marcus's angry look melted somewhat. Then the Traveler spoke these words from The Book.

The Lord God placed the man in the Garden of Eden to tend and care for it.

"You see, my friend," said the Traveler, "from the very beginning you have had this mandate. You must work. God the Creator worked to form this universe, and he still works to sustain it. Yet he cares for you who labor. He himself rested from his work, and he commands rest for his creatures."

Remember to observe the Sabbath day by keeping it holy. Six days a week are set apart for your daily duties and regular work, but the seventh day is a day of rest dedicated to the Lord your God. On that day no one in your household may do any kind of work. This includes you, your sons and daughters, your male and female servants, your livestock, and any foreigners living among you.

"The loving Father who made this weary world and blesses it with good things desires your love and worship. You are to worship him alone, not your work, and not the things you gain from your labor. O people, how many of you worship your work, expecting it to satisfy every want of your eye and your heart? It was not meant to do that. Do you not understand that work and worship are not the same? Do you not see that work for its own sake is folly? Work because you must—you have heard the words from The Book. But take pleasure in your rest also, as The Book tells you." Then the Traveler read these words from The Book.

> I have noticed one thing, at least, that is good. It is good for people to eat well, drink a good glass of wine, and enjoy their work—whatever they do under the sun—for however long God lets them live. And it is a good thing to receive wealth from God and the good health to enjoy it. To enjoy your work and accept your lot in life—that is indeed a gift from God. People who do this rarely look with sorrow on the past, for God has given them reasons for joy.
>
> Never be lazy in your work, but serve the Lord enthusiastically.
>
> This should be your ambition: to live a quiet life, minding your own business and working with your hands, just as we commanded you before. As a result, people who are not Christians will respect the way you live, and you will not need to depend on others to meet your financial needs.

Some of the younger men and women were listening critically, for they did not highly value work, and they knew that for them work was not essential. They lived only for pleasure, and for them every day was a day of rest, though not set aside for worshiping the Lord. Day in and day out, all was an endless round of jollity. And they knew that some of the people who labored hard also envied them. For these people so obsessed with pleasure, the Traveler said these words from The Book.

I said to myself, "Come now, let's give pleasure a try. Let's look for the 'good things' in life." But I found that this, too, was meaningless. "It is silly to be laughing all the time," I said. "What good does it do to seek only pleasure?"

After much thought, I decided to cheer myself with wine. While still seeking wisdom, I clutched at foolishness. In this way, I hoped to experience the only happiness most people find during their brief life in this world.

I bought slaves, both men and women, and others were born into my household. I also owned great herds and flocks, more than any of the kings who lived in Jerusalem before me. I collected great sums of silver and gold, the treasure of many kings and provinces. I hired wonderful singers, both men and women, and had many beautiful concubines. I had everything a man could desire!

So I became greater than any of the kings who ruled in Jerusalem before me. And with it all, I remained clear-eyed so that I could evaluate all these things. Anything I wanted, I took. I did not restrain myself from any joy. I even found great pleasure in hard work, an additional reward for all my labors.

But as I looked at everything I had worked so hard to accomplish, it was all so meaningless. It was like chasing the wind. There was nothing really worthwhile anywhere.

When the Unknown Traveler said these words, some of the young people laughed to themselves. But a few were touched inwardly, for they knew that they, like the one whose words were recorded in The Book, found that pleasure for its own sake was vain and trifling.

The Traveler then spoke further on this.

Destruction is certain for you who get up early to begin long drinking bouts that last late into the night. You furnish lovely music and wine at your grand parties; the harps, lyres, tambourines, and flutes are superb! But you never think about the Lord or notice what he is doing.

But instead, you dance and play; you slaughter sacrificial animals, feast on meat, and drink wine. "Let's eat, drink, and be merry," you say. "What's the difference, for tomorrow we die."

"People of the Valley," the Traveler said, closing The Book, "do not believe for a moment that the God who spangled the sky with multicolored birds and dappled the fields with wildflowers would deny you joy and play. Consider the words of God's Son himself."

My purpose is to give life in all its fullness.
I have told you this so that you will be filled with my joy. Yes, your joy will overflow!

Then the Traveler broke into a radiant smile, and his joy beamed over the square and the people gathered there. His voice was jubilant as he read these words.

Rejoice in the Lord and be glad, all you who obey him! Shout for joy, all you whose hearts are pure!
Happy are those who obey his decrees and search for him with all their hearts.

The words the Traveler had read settled like weights in the hearts and minds of the People of the Valley. But as they pondered them, a flock of brightly colored finches flew over the square, whistling and chattering like a pack of children let out of school. And the People of the Valley could see that the Maker of the universe took delight in his creatures' frolics.

the
BODY

THE HOLLOW eyes and the pallor of some who had wasted themselves showed on the faces of some who were there watching the Unknown Traveler. Among these was a man named Owen, who was only thirty years old, though the lines in his face added another ten years to his look. Owen was not drunk, though he had been the night before. He was glad when clouds covered the sun that day, for bright sunlight stung his eyes.

Some who had wasted themselves were not pale, and their eyes were bright. Yet inwardly—and the wise, some-what like God, see inwardly—these were ugly. For ugliness lies in not being what the Maker of both matter and spirit destined things to be.

The woman Owen lived with was not there. She was

at their dwelling, and Owen hoped she was alone, though he knew this was unlikely. But he was not sure this mattered, for she was not his first woman, and he did not expect her to be his last.

This man had enjoyed his youth to the full, and though he could not ignore the changed face in his mirror, he was unwilling to change the pursuits of his youth. His body, he knew, was not as lean or tight or desirable as it once had been, yet he still perceived it as something to be spent in nothing more than pleasure. And this was how he perceived others. He never lacked for companions who saw the world as he saw it.

But on this particular day his flesh called out for nothing more than a respite. His head and stomach throbbed, one seeming full and the other empty, and what seemed like a fever washed over him every few moments. And so he was in the square, away from his woman and away from the tavern, somehow feeling drawn to this Unknown Traveler and The Book that had been so long forgotten.

A cloud passed over, and Owen's eyes felt some relief at having the sun obscured for a time. The Traveler began to speak to the People of the Valley.

"There is not one blade of grass, there is no color in this world that is not intended to make us rejoice. We are put into this world not only to be spectators in this beautiful theatre, but to enjoy the vast bounty and variety of good things which are offered to us in it. You have eyes and ears and your other senses because the Creator made this infinite variety for his pleasure, and for yours. Yet because selfishness and vanity mar every bit of creation, this flesh you are made of is subject to all kinds of abuses."

Then the Traveler began to read to them from The Book.

When you follow the desires of your sinful nature, your lives will produce these evil results: sexual immorality, impure thoughts, eagerness for lustful pleasure, idolatry, participation in demonic activities, hostility, quarreling, jealousy, outbursts of anger, selfish ambition, divisions, the feeling that everyone is wrong except those in your own little group, envy, drunkenness, wild parties, and other kinds of sin.

You drink wine by the bowlful, and you perfume yourselves with exotic fragrances, caring nothing at all that your nation is going to ruin.

Wine produces mockers; liquor leads to brawls. Whoever is led astray by drink cannot be wise.

How can I pardon you? For even your children have turned from me. They have sworn by gods that are not gods at all! I fed my people until they were fully satisfied. But they thanked me by committing adultery and lining up at the city's brothels. They are well-fed, lusty stallions, each neighing for his neighbor's wife.

For lust is a shameful sin, a crime that should be punished. It is a devastating fire that destroys to hell. It would wipe out everything I own.

You can be sure that no immoral, impure, or greedy person will inherit the Kingdom of Christ and of God. For a greedy person is really an idolater who worships the things of this world.

Don't you know that those who do wrong will have no share in the Kingdom of God? Don't fool yourselves. Those who indulge in sexual sin, who are idol worshipers, adulterers, male prostitutes, homo-sexuals, thieves, greedy people, drunkards, abusers, and swindlers—none of these will have a share in the Kingdom of God.

Don't be fooled by those who try to excuse these sins, for the terrible anger of God comes upon all those who disobey him.

Owen had opened his mouth to speak, but his mind was fogged, and he had no vigor left in him after the previous night. The Traveler continued to read.

Another reason for right living is that you know how late it is; time is running out. Wake up, for the coming of our salvation is nearer now than when we first believed. The night is almost gone; the day of salvation will soon be here.

So don't live in darkness. Get rid of your evil deeds. Shed them like dirty clothes. Clothe yourselves with the armor of right living, as those who live in the light. We should be decent and true in everything we do, so that everyone can approve of our behavior. Don't participate in wild parties and getting drunk, or in adultery and immoral living, or in fighting and jealousy. But let the Lord Jesus Christ take control of you, and don't think of ways to indulge your evil desires.

Follow the steps of good men instead, and stay on the paths of the righteous. For only the upright will live in the land, and those who have integrity will remain in it. But the wicked will be removed from the land, and the treacherous will be destroyed.

With the Lord's authority let me say this: Live no longer as the ungodly do, for they are hopelessly confused. Their closed minds are full of darkness; they are far away from the life of God because they have shut their minds and hardened their hearts against him. They don't care anymore about right and wrong, and they have given themselves over to immoral ways. Their lives are filled with all kinds of impurity and greed.

But that isn't what you were taught when you learned about Christ. Since you have heard all about him and have learned the truth that is in Jesus, throw off your old evil nature and your former way of life, which is rotten through and through, full of lust and deception. Instead, there must be a spiritual renewal of your thoughts and attitudes. You must display a new nature because you are a new person, created in God's likeness—righteous, holy, and true.

You say, "Food is for the stomach, and the stomach is for food." This is true, though someday God will do away with both of them. But our bodies were not made for sexual immorality. They were made for the Lord, and the Lord cares about our bodies.

Run away from sexual sin! No other sin so clearly affects the body as this one does. For sexual immorality is a sin against your own body.

Don't be drunk with wine, because that will ruin your life. Instead, let the Holy Spirit fill and control you.

Don't you know that your body is the temple of the Holy Spirit, who lives in you and was given to you by God? You do not belong to yourself, for God bought you with a high price. So you must honor God with your body.

For though your hearts were once full of darkness, now you are full of light from the Lord, and your behavior should show it! For this light within you produces only what is good and right and true.

A certain woman, who had lived a very clean and sober life, was nodding her head in agreement. She said to the Traveler, "How true this all is. Throughout my life I have watched my companions and my children's companions wasting themselves away. The flesh—that is what pollutes our lives."

But the Traveler shook his head, knowing how humans liked to blame their failings on external things. He began to read again.

It is the thought-life that defiles you. For from within, out of a person's heart, come evil thoughts, sexual immorality, theft, murder, adultery, greed, wickedness, deceit, eagerness for lustful pleasure, envy, slander, pride, and foolishness. All these vile things come from within; they are what defile you and make you unacceptable to God.

There was a time when some of you were just like that, but now your sins have been washed away, and you have been set apart for God. You have been made right with God because of what the Lord Jesus Christ and the Spirit of our God have done for you.

Owen found his voice, and he said to the Traveler, "What The Book tells us is that our lives are not only to be without sin, but without joy. Does God not give us rules to drain all the color out of life? My friends would laugh at me for leading such a life, and they would be right to do so."

The Unknown Traveler said, "No color of the spectrum is denied to those who love God. Pity it is that so many of you assume that the God of heaven despises pleasure and frames rules so that men and women will offend him if they smile. Would he who designed every part of you forbid you to feel joy in it? Will you listen to the words of a man who poured out poetry because his desire had set his mind on fire?"

> I am here in my garden, my treasure, my bride! I gather my myrrh with my spices and eat my honeycomb with my honey. I drink my wine with my milk.
>
> How sweet is your love, my treasure, my bride! How much better it is than wine! Your perfume is more fragrant than the richest of spices. Your lips, my bride, are as sweet as honey. Yes, honey and cream are under your tongue. The scent of your clothing is like that of the mountains and the cedars of Lebanon.
>
> Kiss me again and again, for your love is sweeter than wine.
>
> Oh, feed me with your love—your "raisins" and your "apples"—for I am utterly lovesick!
>
> I am here in my garden, my treasure, my bride! I gather my myrrh with my spices and eat my honey-

comb with my honey. Oh, lover and beloved, eat and drink! Yes, drink deeply of this love!

"These words are from The Book of the Lord. Do you still believe he wants you to close your eyes to this world's pleasures? It is not pleasure that the Almighty despises—it is the abuse of pleasure, worshiping it, pursuing it to the sad neglect of duty and honor. The same hands that rightly caress your husbands and wives, and raise a hearty glass at family feast—these hands were made for other things as well. Let the same hand that burned like fire on the wedding night also bandage the wounds of a friend, lift a fallen one from the gutter, and wipe a tear from a prisoner's face."

And the Traveler began to read again.

When the Holy Spirit controls our lives, he will produce this kind of fruit in us: love, joy, peace, patience, kindness, goodness, faithfulness, gentleness, and self-control.

You have had enough in the past of the evil things that godless people enjoy—their immorality and lust, their feasting and drunkenness and wild parties, and their terrible worship of idols.

Of course, your former friends are very surprised when you no longer join them in the wicked things they do, and they say evil things about you. But just remember that they will have to face God, who will judge everyone, both the living and the dead.

We are citizens of heaven, where the Lord Jesus Christ lives. And we are eagerly waiting for him to return as our Savior. He will take these weak mortal bodies of ours and change them into glorious bodies like his own, using the same mighty power that he will use to conquer everything, everywhere.

Owen pondered these things for a moment. And while he was thinking, one of his drinking companions spoke up. "What kind of God is it that The Book gives witness to? Is he a God only of rules and restrictions? Would a loving God take pleasure in seeing his loved ones tangled up in a web of endless regulations? What about freedom? Must the pleasures of our bodies be bounded, pressed into proper channels? Why can we not do whatever we please, so long as we do not abuse someone?"

The Traveler said, "It is true that rules are not the essence of right living. If the heart of God had windows, you would look inside and not see laws and rules, but love. Yet fathers do make rules, because their children are frail and lack understanding. And God is a father, and he knows your weaknesses, and he knows how easily you slip into bondage to what you think you control."

Then the Traveler read these words from the pen of one who had understood both law and love.

You may say, "I am allowed to do anything." But I reply, "Not everything is good for you." And even though "I am allowed to do anything," I must not become a slave to anything. You say, "Food is for the stomach, and the stomach is for food." This is true, though someday God will do away with both of them. But our bodies were not made for sexual immorality. They were made for the Lord, and the Lord cares about our bodies.

The pallid young man Owen walked away from the square, not in anger at the Traveler or The Book, but at his own flesh that seemed embittered against him. And while his throbbing head murmured to him his need to change his life, the power of habit tugged him homeward, drawing him back into a wearisome cycle of satisfaction and regret.

But Owen's companion stayed to hear more, for no one had ever spoken before about how God, dwelling as the Holy Spirit within a man, could bring about transformation.

Seeing that the People of the Valley yearned for words of comfort, the Traveler read these words.

Fix your thoughts on what is true and honorable and right. Think about things that are pure and lovely and admirable. Think about things that are excellent and worthy of praise.

Whatever is good and perfect comes to us from God above, who created all heaven's lights. Unlike them, he never changes or casts shifting shadows.

Everything is pure to those whose hearts are pure. But nothing is pure to those who are corrupt and unbelieving, because their minds and consciences are defiled.

Dear brothers and sisters, I plead with you to give your bodies to God. Let them be a living and holy sacrifice—the kind he will accept. When you think of what he has done for you, is this too much to ask? Don't copy the behavior and customs of this world, but let God transform you into a new person by changing the way you think. Then you will know what God wants you to do, and you will know how good and pleasing and perfect his will really is.

Because we have these promises, dear friends, let us cleanse ourselves from everything that can defile our body or spirit. And let us work toward complete purity because we fear God.

A man in midlife, a man who knew the world's patterns, was listening. He had changed much in recent years. He was not angry or guilty over his past, but he was a faithful student of it. After many years he had learned to politely decline the things that once seemed irresistible. And his family rejoiced, and he rejoiced. He said to the

Traveler, "Once God signs his name across a man's heart, the signature burns through to every particle of him. His days of living for only himself are doomed, and every grain of him is marked for God. And he will sleep well at night only when he makes good on his dedication. When body and soul join in one grand effort for the Lord, the man will sleep the sleep of the just." And many who knew the man well nodded their agreement.

Then the Traveler dismissed them all, for it was the middle of the day. And he asked them to go to their homes, and to eat and drink and be glad that the Maker of heaven and earth had given them their senses. Within himself he prayed that they would ponder the words they had just heard and remember that they need not be mere slaves to their desires.

JUSTICE
AND
LAW

THE VALLEY had its laws and those who served to carry out the laws. And the Valley was no different from any other place, for in it were some people who hated laws because they despised all authority. Yet some hated the laws because justice was not easily had. And abuse of justice, like storm and fire and untimely death, is no less painful because it is inevitable.

Throughout the centuries, spattered as they are with innocent blood, the philosophers and the prophets have puzzled over man's chafing at what is unavoidable. They have asked why a people prone to falseness and evil would shed tears at what they and their kindred brought into being. And the philosophers reach no conclusions, though some say that people remember a time when no falseness marred the face of earth. And some say that what acts in the brain made feverish by injustice is not remembrance, but vision, the vision of a time or place when the inequities will be planed away. The arguments continue, and the yoke of falseness still weighs upon the neck of humanity.

Of those who returned to the square that afternoon were some who carried out the laws. And far from them, though listening with no less interest to the Unknown Traveler's words, were those who had been wounded by the laws. And some of these had been wounded justly, for it is in the scheme of things that true criminals do sometimes receive what they deserve. But some of the wounded ones were victims, for victims are found in every place. Even where sacrifices are not burned on altars, sacrifices there are.

Lara, a woman whose husband was in prison, was thinking of the God of heaven. She was considering whether the lofty One, the One who formed the elements and the laws that govern them, took note of the endless round of making rules, breaking rules, subverting rules, perverting justice—until the innocent and the gullible despaired of truth ever raising its gasping head above the flood of falsehood.

And Lara, whose voice was hard, though it had not always been so, spoke to the Traveler.

"Speak to us of justice—if The Book has anything to say about it."

Then the Traveler began to read these words to show them that equity was never far from the heart of God.

The Lord despises those who acquit the guilty and condemn the innocent.

The Traveler knew that these would be hollow words for some, so he read these words to assure the people that God indeed took note of soured justice.

Destruction is certain for those who drag their sins behind them, tied with cords of falsehood. They even mock the Holy One of Israel and say, "Hurry up and do something! Quick, show us what you can do. We want to see what you have planned."

Destruction is certain for those who say that evil is good and good is evil; that dark is light and light is dark; that bitter is sweet and sweet is bitter.

Perceiving that these words pinched the people's minds, the Traveler continued.

Throughout the world there is evil in the courtroom. Yes, even the courts of law are corrupt!

For our sins are piled up before God and testify against us. Yes, we know what sinners we are. We know that we have rebelled against the Lord. We have turned our backs on God. We know how unfair and oppressive we have been, carefully planning our deceitful lies. Our courts oppose people who are righteous, and justice is nowhere to be found. Truth falls dead in the streets, and fairness has been outlawed. Yes, truth is gone, and anyone who tries to live a godly life is soon attacked.

The Lord looked and was displeased to find that there was no justice.

The leaders of his people trampled prisoners underfoot. They deprived people of their God-given rights in defiance of the Most High. They perverted justice in the courts. Do they think the Lord didn't see it?

You wicked people! You twist justice, making it a bitter pill for the poor and oppressed. Righteousness and fair play are meaningless fictions to you.

How you hate honest judges! How you despise people who tell the truth! You trample the poor and steal what little they have through taxes and unfair rent. Therefore, you will never live in the beautiful stone houses you are building. You will never drink wine from the lush vineyards you are planting. For I know the vast number of your sins and rebellions. You oppress good people by taking bribes and deprive the poor of justice in the courts.

They go about their evil deeds with both hands. How skilled they are at using them! Officials and judges alike demand bribes. The people with money and influence pay them off, and together they scheme to twist justice.

Then the Traveler gazed into the severe face of Lara. Her eyes were blue, but not a youthful blue, the blue of flowers and summer horizons and gemstones. Hers were a faded, pained blue, like old linen grown rawer and rougher from too much washing.

Lara stood next to her friend, a woman her own age, a friend whose eyes were not hard but compassionate. And the Traveler spoke these words, for they gave expression to her friend's voiceless eyes.

Must I forever see this sin and misery all around me? Wherever I look, I see destruction and violence. I am surrounded by people who love to argue and fight. The law has become paralyzed and useless, and there is no justice given in the courts. The wicked far outnumber the righteous, and justice is perverted with bribes and trickery.

"People of the Valley," the Traveler said, "the God of heaven and all who honor him know that this fragmented world's laws are only shadows of laws more binding and more enduring. Every law, and every maker of laws, answers not to the petty written rules that change from one city to another. All must answer to a higher law, and to the One who ordered the world and everything in it."

It is wrong to show favoritism when passing judgment. A judge who says to the wicked, "You are innocent," will be cursed by many people and denounced by the nations. But blessings are showered on those who convict the guilty.

It is wrong for a judge to favor the guilty or condemn the innocent.

Showing partiality is never good, yet some will do wrong for something as small as a piece of bread.

Do not twist justice against people simply because they are poor.

Always judge your neighbors fairly, neither favoring the poor nor showing deference to the rich.

Take no bribes, for a bribe makes you ignore something that you clearly see. A bribe always hurts the cause of the person who is in the right.

Do not oppress the foreigners living among you. You know what it is like to be a foreigner. Remember your own experience in the land of Egypt.

Do not cheat or rob anyone. Always pay your hired workers promptly. Show your fear of God by treating the deaf with respect and by not taking advantage of the blind. I am the Lord.

Give fair judgment to the poor and the orphan;

uphold the rights of the oppressed and the destitute. Rescue the poor and helpless; deliver them from the grasp of evil people.

The friend of Lara knew that there could never be justice in the land unless the people pursued the Truth with a passion. And then the Traveler read these words about the Truth.

Keep far away from falsely charging anyone with evil. Never put an innocent or honest person to death. I will not allow anyone guilty of this to go free.

Do not pass along false reports. Do not cooperate with evil people by telling lies on the witness stand.

Do not join a crowd that intends to do evil. When you are on the witness stand, do not be swayed in your testimony by the opinion of the majority. And do not slant your testimony in favor of a person just because that person is poor.

Some of the People of the Valley took heart at these words, but others scoffed to themselves, for they knew that every rule, whether from God or man, would be trampled in the mud in the name of selfishness. And for the scoffers, who understood a portion of the Truth, the Traveler read these words.

If you see a poor person being oppressed by the powerful and justice being miscarried throughout the land, don't be surprised! For every official is under orders from higher up, and matters of justice only get lost in red tape and bureaucracy.

"Dear people, those who oppress and who are oppressed, never cease to believe in the just One who rules. And never cease to pray for the ones bearing the burden for meting out justice. You curse them, and you covet their power and their gains, but neither is right. You end by wallowing in your spite and envy. Pray for them, asking your Creator to lessen the weight of injustice on the victims." And he read them this prayer.

Give justice to the king, O God, and righteousness to the king's son. Help him judge your people in the right way; let the poor always be treated fairly. May the mountains yield prosperity for all, and may the hills be fruitful, because the king does what is right. Help him to defend the poor, to rescue the children of the needy, and to crush their oppressors. May he live as long as the sun shines, as long as the moon continues in the skies. Yes, forever!

Standing against a pillar in the square were two brothers, hardly out of their boyhood. And they were full of malice, for they saw before them daily the workings of inequity, yet they could not see the God of heaven, and they doubted his concern for justice. Often the anger that only youth can feel pricked their insides like a holly's thorns. And when the Traveler spoke of praying for the keepers of the law, one of the brothers laughed.

"What do we owe the ones whose rules break our backs? There are others who could bring more fairness to the Valley." And he spoke loudly, hoping the officials would see him and take note. Hatred, when it is on fire, sheds its anonymity.

The Traveler, knowing that youth and those with the minds of youth despise all authority but themselves, read them this story of the Son of God.

> The Pharisees met together to think of a way to trap Jesus into saying something for which they could accuse him. They decided to send some of their disciples, along with the supporters of Herod, to ask him this question: "Teacher, we know how honest you are. You teach about the way of God regardless of the consequences. You are impartial and don't play favorites. Now tell us what you think about this: Is it right to pay taxes to the Roman government or not?"
>
> But Jesus knew their evil motives. "You hypocrites!" he said. "Whom are you trying to fool with your trick questions? Here, show me the Roman coin

used for the tax." When they handed him the coin, he asked, "Whose picture and title are stamped on it?"

"Caesar's," they replied.

"Well, then," he said, "give to Caesar what belongs to him. But everything that belongs to God must be given to God."

"Do you think," the Traveler asked, "that this Caesar, this emperor of the world, received unbroken praise from all his subjects? Do you not know that the peace laid upon the land by the callous and insolent Romans was bought at the cost of a hundred rivers of blood and a measureless expanse of a nation's dignity? Like every king who ever had a knee bowed to him, this emperor committed both good and bad, and how well the Son of God must have known that this was so." Then the Traveler read these words.

Obey the government, for God is the one who put it there. All governments have been placed in power by God. So those who refuse to obey the laws of the land are refusing to obey God, and punishment will follow.

Pay your taxes, too, for these same reasons. For government workers need to be paid so they can keep on doing the work God intended them to do.

Give to everyone what you owe them: Pay your taxes
and import duties, and give respect and honor to all
to whom it is due.

You are not slaves; you are free. But your freedom
is not an excuse to do evil. You are free to live as
God's slaves. Show respect for everyone. Love your
Christian brothers and sisters. Fear God. Show
respect for the king.

At hearing this, the two angry brothers walked away.
For they could not then believe that the God spoken of in
The Book truly cared for the poor and the downtrodden.

And some of the other people there, both young and
not young, were with them in spirit. Raw youth possess the
vigor for revolt, but so often they are cheered on by their
staid elders, who remember well their own earlier rebellion
and how noble it feels to yell and hurl mud at fattened, lazy
officials. So some elders took pleasure in seeing the two
brothers, like young leopards clawing the turf, wailing for
prey.

But some people took the Traveler's words to heart.
Martin did, though part of him doubted that Almighty God
intended men to obey evil rulers and not question them. So
Martin spoke for himself and for others and said to the Traveler, "Is it ever right and proper to disobey? We understand
that the One who ordered everything, even order itself,
wishes to keep us from the fear and despair of anarchy. And

we know it is right to obey the laws and to pray for those who make them. But is it always possible? When the Son of God told us to give God what belongs to God, surely he knew that doing one may hinder us from the other."

The Traveler said, "Dear people, Jesus, the Son of God, while he walked this earth, used his power to heal many people. After he departed this world, his followers did many of the same miracles, as he told them they would. And for proclaiming God's truth to the people, the people who had for centuries awaited the Son of God's coming, the two men were jailed. And the people's Council, the very ones who should have welcomed the Son of God and his followers, brought them to trial." Then the Traveler read these words.

> Peter and John replied, "Do you think God wants us to obey you rather than him? We cannot stop telling about the wonderful things we have seen and heard."

And Martin understood more than he had before. But he and all the people there were still perplexed, for they despaired over real justice ever reigning on the earth. And so the Traveler gave them assurance, for he could taste their anguish in the autumn air.

> In due season God will judge everyone, both good and bad, for all their deeds.

God presides over heaven's court; he pronounces judgment on the judges.

"People, you will never see true justice in this world. You may have the vision of it—indeed, you must have that vision always burning within you—but you will not see it brought to pass. It cannot be so. This world's journal is a long and tedious tale of one king followed by another, one more just than the next, the other a little less so, then a dynasty toppled by another, judging the cruelties of the first, yet engendering its own. A crown and a scepter are buried, and the one who wore them is cursed, but the new commander makes a crown for himself, and others envy him, and they wait their chance, and the pitiful tale goes on. But do not believe that only the poor are afflicted in this tale. Rich and poor alike suffer, oppressors and oppressed are wounded, injustice blights both the abased and their governors. No one who draws breath is untouched. And those who plot one revolution after another only fool themselves for a time. And while you struggle against the wrong, do not believe you will ever root it out. It is stronger than you. Yet believe in this One who will bring the right to the fore." Then the Traveler read sobering words to the People of the Valley.

Dear brothers and sisters, you are foreigners and aliens here. So I warn you to keep away from evil desires because they fight against your very souls.

But this is what you must do: Tell the truth to each other. Render verdicts in your courts that are just and that lead to peace.

God blesses those who are hungry and thirsty for justice,
for they will receive it in full.
God blesses those who are merciful,
for they will be shown mercy.
God blesses those whose hearts are pure,
for they will see God.
God blesses those who work for peace,
for they will be called the children of God.
God blesses those who are persecuted because they live for God,
for the Kingdom of Heaven is theirs.

Lara, the woman whose husband was in prison, raised up her eyes to heaven and prayed that the Lord, the Judge of all the earth, would pour out his peace upon every victim. And Martin, who knew her, and who bled inside for her, prayed also for those who practice injustice. He prayed that they would remember those they had abused. He longed for them to recall the One whose just rule they had ignored. And he prayed for the Kingdom and its inhabitants, who now seemed out of place in the world.

And so both oppressor and oppressed were brought before the just and merciful God in prayer that day.

WORSHIP

A MAN named Terence, a widower, had had a wife for many years who prayed often and talked constantly of her love for God. And Terence had been sometimes amused and sometimes admiring. And now, these many years after her passing, he wondered what it was that had moved her daily to testify to her love for God.

He asked the Traveler, "What is worship?"

The Traveler replied, "Worship is recognizing that love draws boundaries. It is acknowledging that the great Lover, the one who exists to give love and to be loved, is jealous, as any devoted lover rightfully is. Worship is saying to God, the Lover, 'We belong to each other, you and I, and whatever else I care for, I care for it less than for you.' Hear what The Book says."

Do not worship any other gods besides me.

Do not make idols of any kind, whether in the shape of birds or animals or fish. You must never worship or bow down to them, for I, the Lord your God, am a jealous God who will not share your affection with any other god! I do not leave unpunished the sins of those who hate me, but I punish the children for the sins of their parents to the third and fourth generations.

Those who trust in idols, calling them their gods—they will be turned away in shame.

Those who chase after other gods will be filled with sorrow. I will not take part in their sacrifices or even speak the names of their gods.

Dear children, keep away from anything that might take God's place in your hearts.

We have come to bring you the Good News that you should turn from these worthless things to the living God, who made heaven and earth, the sea, and everything in them.

"Understand," the Traveler said, "that idols are more than images of stone or clay. Whatever you bow down to, whatever your heart salutes as its master, that is an idol. All that exists, exists because God, the one Center of the universe, made it. And only that Center merits your full devotion. He alone deserves your songs of gratitude and the daily bending of your hearts toward him."

Terence spoke again. "This God, this Great Being who made all, who gave being to whatever is—can we indeed approach him as if we are speaking to a lover or a friend? Is not One so mighty and so pure too far from us to be approached?"

"One who is truly mighty can stoop down," the Traveler said. "The ruler of a nation bows down to hear the muddled words of his small grandson. And though we know the Lord God is greater than anyone, yet we cannot cower in fear when we are overwhelmed with gratitude." Then the Traveler began to read.

This is the day the Lord has made. We will rejoice and be glad in it.

Praise the Lord, I tell myself; with my whole heart, i will praise his holy name. Praise the Lord, I tell myself, and never forget the good things he does for me.

He ransoms me from death and surrounds me with love and tender mercies. He fills my life with good things. My youth is renewed like the eagle's!

Acknowledge that the Lord is God! He made us, and we are his. We are his people, the sheep of his pasture.

Give glory to him. For the time has come when he will sit as judge. Worship him who made heaven and earth, the sea, and all the springs of water.

Come, let us worship and bow down. Let us kneel before the Lord our maker.

Shout with joy to the Lord, O earth! worship the Lord with gladness. Come before him, singing with joy.

Enter his gates with thanksgiving; go into his courts with praise. Give thanks to him and bless his name. For the Lord is good. His unfailing love continues forever, and his faithfulness continues to each generation.

A woman standing near Terence had a conscience that bore a ponderous load, and she believed she could not draw near to Almighty God, no matter how grateful she might be. She had learned what a burden and an ache it was to commit offenses and not have them forgiven. She asked the Traveler, "Can one who has done what God the Great Being condemns ever bow down to him? Will he not leave us in the dust, wallowing in the refuse of our past?"

The Unknown Traveler warmed at beholding a heart that could feel its unworthiness. He read these words, looking deep into the woman's eyes.

Who may climb the mountain of the Lord? Who may stand in his holy place? Only those whose hands and hearts are pure, who do not worship idols and never tell lies.

They will receive the Lord's blessing and have right

standing with God their Savior. They alone may enter God's presence and worship the God of Israel.

So wherever you assemble, I want men to pray with holy hands lifted up to God, free from anger and controversy.

He could see the birthing of a tear in the woman's eye, for what he had read to her was no consolation. She did not feel her heart was clean or her hands holy. And he read again.

Day and night your hand of discipline was heavy on me. My strength evaporated like water in the summer heat.

For troubles surround me—too many to count! They pile up so high I can't see my way out. They are more numerous than the hairs on my head. I have lost all my courage.

Finally, I confessed all my sins to you and stopped trying to hide them. I said to myself, "I will confess my rebellion to the Lord." And you forgave me! All my guilt is gone.

"O Lord," I prayed, "have mercy on me. Heal me, for I have sinned against you."

He forgives all my sins and heals all my diseases. He ransoms me from death and surrounds me with love and tender mercies.

Therefore, let all the godly confess their rebellion to you while there is time, that they may not drown in the floodwaters of judgment.

Oh, what joy for those whose rebellion is forgiven, whose sin is put out of sight! Yes, what joy for those whose record the Lord has cleared of sin, whose lives are lived in complete honesty!

Now the repentant woman's one tear had joined with many others. She withdrew from the square, not in anger and not in shame, but in the sad joy that requires time and space by itself, time to linger awhile with God the Forgiver. The woman with the sad joy had not known that mere words could so rain on a dry heart. Yet she was pleased that the God who endowed his creatures with words could so delightfully use them himself.

Terence remembered how his wife had many times walked in the forest near the Valley, sometimes seeming lost in thoughts, sometimes with glad eyes gazing at the ancient pines and the carpet of verdant moss. And he had sometimes followed her, though not so close as to disturb her. And he had heard her singing to the One who gave such joy. Now Terence asked the Traveler, "Our worship of God is a solitary act, is it not?"

The Traveler replied, "Every heart is solitary before the Almighty, for everyone must by himself account for his deeds and misdeeds. How right, how proper it is for everyone to review in his heart throughout the day the good things God has bestowed. Yet how much joy there is in gathering together in a body, proving that there are others who have not forgotten this world's Maker and Redeemer, though it sometimes seems that all the world slights him." Then he read these words.

Where two or three gather together because they are mine, I am there among them.

Let us not neglect our meeting together, as some people do, but encourage and warn each other, especially now that the day of his coming back again is drawing near.

He is the God who made the world and everything in it. Since he is Lord of heaven and earth, he doesn't live in man-made temples, and human hands can't serve his needs—for he has no needs. He himself gives life and breath to everything, and he satisfies every need there is.

A man who wore garments carefully chosen was a collector of paintings and sculptures. He prided himself on his love of beauty, and he was pleased whenever the Traveler spoke of how the Creator had formed the great and the small things of the universe and set them together in patterns of delight. He spoke to the Traveler, saying, "Sir, nothing in the world could be more glorious than for people to gather together and sing proper hymns and recite words from The Book with great dignity. How the Creator must be honored when he beholds the beauty and the measured graciousness of ritual and our holy days. And how he must savor our raising up stately buildings in his honor."

The Traveler nodded, yet he did not smile at this. "This is truth, but it lacks. There is more." Then he read these words from The Book.

I hate all your show and pretense—the hypocrisy of your religious festivals and solemn assemblies. I will not accept your burnt offerings and grain offerings. I won't even notice all your choice peace offerings. Away with your hymns of praise! They are only noise to my ears. I will not listen to your music, no matter how lovely it is.

Even now in your holy festivals, you don't think about me but only of pleasing yourselves.

Smooth words may hide a wicked heart, just as a pretty glaze covers a common clay pot.

The Lord says, "These people say they are mine. they honor me with their lips, but their hearts are far away. And their worship of me amounts to nothing more than human laws learned by rote.

Instead, I want to see a mighty flood of justice, a river of righteous living that will never run dry.

The Most High doesn't live in temples made by human hands. As the prophet says, "Heaven is my throne, and the earth is my footstool. Could you ever build me a temple as good as that?" asks the Lord. "Could you build a dwelling place for me?"

The time is coming and is already here when true worshipers will worship the Father in spirit and in truth. The Father is looking for anyone who will worship him that way. For God is Spirit, so those who worship him must worship in spirit and in truth.

Then the Unknown Traveler read these words of the Son of God so the people would remember that they could not worship without loving each other.

If you are standing before the altar in the Temple, offering a sacrifice to God, and you suddenly remember that someone has something against you, leave your sacrifice there beside the altar. Go and be reconciled to that person. Then come and offer your sacrifice to God.

"People of the Valley," said the Traveler in a pleading tone, "in this bewildered world, men and women worship their work, work at their play, and play at their worship. And this should not be. Your worship of the Ruler of the universe is not to be theatre. Worship is to pour forth out of you like the language of love. It is a mingling of praise, adoration, appeals, sorrow over mistakes, and forgiveness for them, like the father and child at their finest. And worship is the embrace that only reconciled lovers can know. When it occurs, there is nothing like it in this world. It is a sip from the cup of heaven."

JOY

MADELINE was a woman who had practiced at being sad. Like everyone in the Valley, she had endured sickness, worried over her children, and borne all manner of disappointments. Yet though she had had no more rain or pain than most, her great delight seemed to be in recounting her lack of delight. Some who knew her pitied her, which is what she wished. Sad people's single happiness is found in being observed in their sadness. But others considered her nothing more than a nurse for her own wounds.

The young ones in the Valley brought sneers to Madeline's downturned mouth. They, she believed, understood little of the hurts of this world, and she knew their laughter arose from a false and trivial view of life. Like most carriers of gloom, she could not imagine that real joy existed. Madeline believed all laughter was only a mask covering a ceaseless scream—a scream at a universe bent on vexing and perplexing its inhabitants. And the more robust the laughter, she thought, the more pitiful the internal wailing.

Martin, who had been the first of the People of the Valley to meet the Unknown Traveler, knew Madeline. He perceived how she saw life through a cruel lens, knew that to see things as she saw them was to waste one's eyes. Yet on the days when bad had clearly triumphed over good in his life, he understood her, and why her heart had wrapped dark bandages around itself.

Martin said to the Traveler, "What cause is there to be happy in this world?" And he asked this not with the tone of a young scholar striving to look grave, but with the tone of a man asking a question men should ask.

Then the Traveler replied, "Have you not felt a baby's soft cheek against your own? Have you not known the wave that washes through you when your wife's lips touch your tired neck? Have you not cried those peculiar, exquisite tears when you walked in a misty meadow at sunset and felt that the larks' song and the violets' blossoms had been put there for your liking? Have you not lain in your warm bed on a snowy night and remembered the evening's banquet, with food and drink to spare?

"Have you not heard a man awkward in love, suddenly dripping poetry from his mouth because a woman's embrace had fired his soul? Have you not heard a singer pouring out a rhapsody that seemed to trickle down from heaven? Have you not passed through your doorway and been greeted by the smell of fresh-baked bread? Have you never marveled at a falcon hovering over a summer field? Have you never stood at a window with your hands on your children's shoulders, watching the waters of March trickling across the stones of the street?"

And Martin said, "We have all known these things, and more besides. Yet sometimes we pause in the midst of laughter, in the midst of loving, in the midst of bouncing a giggling child on our knees. We pause, and for a moment the sweetness slackens, and we wonder why it is we take joy in these things."

"And have you ever," asked the Traveler, "questioned the joy you felt in God, Almighty God?" Then he picked up The Book and read these words.

> This is a sacred day before our Lord. Don't be dejected and sad, for the joy of the Lord is your strength!
>
> Serve the Lord with reverent fear, and rejoice with trembling.

Then the Traveler paused, and seeing anticipation in Martin's face, he continued with these words of one who loved God.

You have given me greater joy than those who have abundant harvests of grain and wine.

I will be filled with joy because of you. I will sing praises to your name, O Most High.

The law of the Lord is perfect, reviving the soul. the decrees of the Lord are trustworthy, making wise the simple. The commandments of the Lord are right, bringing joy to the heart. The commands of the Lord are clear, giving insight to life.

Your words are what sustain me. They bring me great joy and are my heart's delight, for I bear your name, O Lord God Almighty.

A river brings joy to the city of our God, the sacred home of the Most High.

"Does it seem so strange to you, dear friends, to sing of joy in God? Through ages and ages men had made rhymes and sung songs about the sweetness of love, the comforts of hearth and home, the beauties of trees and flowers, the glories of victory in battle. And this is right. Yet how the soul is stirred by the joy of God! No song ever sung for lover or homeland compares with the anthems that have come from the minds of those animated by holy joy. You have heard the sweetest anthems ever sung poured forth from those whose hearts were spent. They sang, despaired, and almost died. Then they clutched God, and sang an even sweeter song." And when the Traveler had said this, he began to read again.

> Let all who take refuge in you rejoice; let them sing joyful praises forever. Protect them, so all who love your name may be filled with joy.
>
> I trust in your unfailing love. I will rejoice because you have rescued me.
>
> You feed them from the abundance of your own house, letting them drink from your rivers of delight.
>
> I lie awake thinking of you, meditating on you through the night. I think how much you have helped me; I sing for joy in the shadow of your protecting wings.
>
> Happy are people of integrity, who follow the law of the Lord. Happy are those who obey his decrees and search for him with all their hearts. They do not compromise with evil, and they walk only in his paths.
>
> Shout, O earth! Break forth into song, O mountains and forests and every tree!

When the Traveler spoke these words, he lifted his eyes from the pages, and his face shone with elation.

Madeline's cloud, invisible, yet thicker than the gray clouds of autumn that hung over the Valley that day, had not dispersed. But she had been touched by what Martin said to the Traveler. Martin, it seemed, was a perplexed inquirer, unsure that all the questions of his youth had been answered. And Madeline was past asking questions, for she had pronounced the universe ugly and hostile.

But even those who are decided and fixed can sometimes raise questions. And that is what Madeline did on that day.

"Sir, is it possible that our joy in this world is diminished by our yearning for something greater?" And to assure the Traveler that what she asked was not merely selfish and childish, she continued. "I mean to say, were we created for something else than this world, beautiful though it is? We love to look upon beauty, but something—or someone—calls us not to observe, but to unite. We want not only to see, but to live with, and live in, and be lost in. And this eludes us."

Those standing near Madeline stared in disbelief, for they had never heard her speak well of anything. They had known for years that even when the cherry trees in the Valley burst forth in pink vestments, Madeline's countenance was not altered. But Martin understood her, for he knew that underneath the bitterness was someone who dreamed of noble and enduring things.

The Traveler understood her also. And he read these words.

> Those who have been ransomed by the Lord will return to Jerusalem, singing songs of everlasting joy. Sorrow and mourning will disappear, and they will be overcome with joy and gladness.

You will live in joy and peace. The mountains and hills will burst into song, and the trees of the field will clap their hands!

Even the wilderness will rejoice in those days. The desert will blossom with flowers. Yes, there will be an abundance of flowers and singing and joy! The deserts will become as green as the mountains of Lebanon, as lovely as Mount Carmel's pastures and the plain of Sharon. There the Lord will display his glory, the splendor of our God.

Rejoice greatly, O people of Zion! Shout in triumph, O people of Jerusalem! Look, your king is coming to you.

Then he paused and said, "I have more to say to you of what is to come—what lies beyond this world, and what awaits you." And so that he would not leave them merely perplexed, he read them this command, one of the sublimest ever written, one most joyous to execute.

You will sing psalms and hymns and spiritual songs among yourselves, making music to the Lord in your hearts.

And even those who scoffed at the notion of God were pleased to hear that God commanded music of his beloved ones.

the
FUTURE

MARTIN had an old uncle who lived on an immense estate
in the Valley. He was a hardened, bitter man, a man whose
legacy in the world was a massive fortune of wealth—and a
vast desert of feeling. This old man cared little for anyone.
Every person on this earth suffers, at certain seasons, from an
eclipse of the heart, but Martin's old uncle had chosen to
lodge perpetually in the darkness.

Members of his family had tried for years to break
through the hard husk he had formed around himself.
Martin hoped that some change might occur before the old
man faced the prospect of dying.

On this day the old uncle was there, though he gave
little credence to the Unknown Traveler and to The Book
from which he had read. But he did listen as an arrogant

young man stepped forward and spoke with an abrasive tone to the Traveler.

"Sir, you have spoken to us time and time again about this loving Father who creates us and rescues us. How could one so full of love allow his beloved creatures to perish? These silly rumors of punishment are not to be taken seriously, are they? Are they not mere fabrications of parents trying to invoke fear in unruly children?"

The Traveler looked around the square, perceiving that even some gray-haired grandparents were still, in some ways, unruly children. And he knew that so many People of the Valley lived in the realm of wishful thinking, unwilling to face the painful truths of existence. He read them these words from The Book, knowing that some would laugh, for men may whistle in graveyards and laugh at a vision of judgment.

> The hope of the godless comes to nothing. Everything they count on will collapse. They are leaning on a spiderweb. They cling to their home for security, but it won't last. They try to hold it fast, but it will not endure.
>
> The godless seem so strong, like a lush plant growing in the sunshine, its branches spreading across the garden. Its roots grow down through a pile of rocks to hold it firm. But when it is uprooted, it isn't even missed! That is the end of its life, and others spring up from the earth to replace it.

Martin's old uncle shifted his weight onto his heels as he listened. He liked the words of the arrogant youth who had spoken. But there was a stinging truth in the words of the Traveler.

"All lovers must come to dust. All of you are lovers of something or someone—yourselves, or what you used to be, or your possessions, or the dream of having possessions. What becomes of the thing you love is what will become of you. That is why The Book tells you, line after line, to love the One Being who made all things—for love will not come to dust."

Notice how God is both kind and severe. He is severe to those who disobeyed, but kind to you as you continue to trust in his kindness. But if you stop trusting, you also will be cut off.

Don't you realize that whatever you choose to obey becomes your master? You can choose sin, which leads to death, or you can choose to obey God and receive his approval.

The eyes of the Lord watch over those who do right, and his ears are open to their prayers. But the Lord turns his face against those who do evil.

Don't you know that those who do wrong will have no share in the Kingdom of God? Don't fool yourselves. Those who indulge in sexual sin, who are idol worshipers, adulterers, male prostitutes, homo-sexuals, thieves, greedy people, drunkards, abusers, and swindlers—none of these will have a share in the Kingdom of God.

You can be sure that no immoral, impure, or greedy person will inherit the Kingdom of Christ and of God. For a greedy person is really an idolater who worships the things of this world. Don't be fooled by those who try to excuse these sins, for the terrible anger of God comes upon all those who disobey him.

For the truth about God is known to them instinctively. God has put this knowledge in their hearts. From the time the world was created, people have seen the earth and sky and all that God made. They can clearly see his invisible qualities—his eternal power and divine nature. So they have no excuse whatsoever for not knowing God.

There is no judgment awaiting those who trust him. But those who do not trust him have already been judged for not believing in the only Son of God. Their judgment is based on this fact: The light from heaven came into the world, but they loved the darkness more than the light, for their actions were evil. They hate the light because they want to sin in the darkness. They stay away from the light for fear their sins will be exposed and they will be punished.

There is going to come a day of judgment when God, the just judge of all the world, will judge all people according to what they have done. He will pour out his anger and wrath on those who live for themselves, who refuse to obey the truth and practice evil deeds.

Martin's old uncle noticed that as the Traveler continued speaking, the arrogant young man withdrew from the square and went to his home. The old man wanted to do the same, but he could not move. Though his heart was old, there was still hope within it, and he waited, wanting the Traveler to speak words of comfort and hope to those who had wasted the years God had given them. But before the comfort came the harder edge of the Truth.

"Do you think," the Traveler asked, "that God wishes to scare you into loving him and giving yourselves to him? No, indeed. The holy risk that God has taken is this: He made you all, knowing you could love him—or reject him. Love given unwillingly is not love. You cannot be yanked into God's Kingdom, yet you can be coaxed by his love. And I would do you wrong not to tell you of the consequences of not loving the Lover.

"What is hell? You see images of flame and an abyss and horrid smells. All are true, for these are pictures of anyone who says, 'I am my own.' You have all known people who already seemed to be in hell, smoldering in their self-interest. With no joy do I speak about these things, yet I must. I do not lie, The Book does not lie.

Those who spend this life cocooned in themselves will surely enter the next life in the same way. Can you bear to think of this—no tomorrows, no plans, no rest, no possibilities. Only a loveless forever and forever without end."

You lived in this world without God and without hope.

God so loved the world that he gave his only Son, so that everyone who believes in him will not perish but have eternal life. God did not send his Son into the world to condemn it, but to save it.

Anyone who believes and is baptized will be saved. But anyone who refuses to believe will be condemned.

Now your sins have been washed away, and you have been set apart for God. You have been made right with God because of what the Lord Jesus Christ and the Spirit of our God have done for you. For though your hearts were once full of darkness, now you are full of light from the Lord, and your behavior should show it!

So now we can rejoice in our wonderful new relationship with God—all because of what our Lord Jesus Christ has done for us in making us friends of God.

For we died and were buried with Christ by baptism. And just as Christ was raised from the dead by the glorious power of the Father, now we also may live new lives.

Just as death came into the world through a man,
Adam, now the resurrection from the dead has begun
through another man, Christ. Everyone dies because
all of us are related to Adam, the first man. But all
who are related to Christ, the other man, will be
given new life.

One old man, a man who had once been a close
companion of Martin's uncle, was warmed when he heard
these words. He had lived a life of kindness and compassion. Though he was loved by all who knew him, he was
worn out from living. As he felt his feeble heart drumming
faintly within him, he longed to hear what life would be
like after this one had passed away.

"Traveler," he said, his voice hardly more than a
whisper, "tell us what we will be like in the next world."

The Traveler began to speak again.

When this earthly tent we live in is taken down—
when we die and leave these bodies—we will have a
home in heaven, an eternal body made for us by God
himself and not by human hands. We grow weary in
our present bodies, and we long for the day when we
will put on our heavenly bodies like new clothing.

Our dying bodies make us groan and sigh, but it's
not that we want to die and have no bodies at all.
We want to slip into our new bodies so that these

dying bodies will be swallowed up by everlasting life. God himself has prepared us for this, and as a guarantee he has given us his Holy Spirit.

So we are always confident, even though we know that as long as we live in these bodies we are not at home with the Lord.

For this world is not our home; we are looking forward to our city in heaven, which is yet to come.

I pray that your hearts will be flooded with light so that you can understand the wonderful future he has promised to those he called. I want you to realize what a rich and glorious inheritance he has given to his people.

You do this because you are looking forward to the joys of heaven—as you have been ever since you first heard the truth of the Good News.

Martin had been observing his uncle's face, and he could see that the Traveler's words were moving the old man. He was not surprised when the old man spoke up.

"How can we be certain? I have lived more than eighty years, and I have seen good men and bad men buried. Do we have any assurance that the good will endure?"

The Traveler said, "What assurance can I give you? I cannot write out a guarantee for you. If you cannot believe that the Son of God was raised up from death, you will not believe that anyone else will be raised up. But in a universe

where an executed carpenter can rise from the dead,
anything is possible. Listen closely to the testimony of one
who believed."

> You will not leave my soul among the dead or allow
> your godly one to rot in the grave. You will show me
> the way of life, granting me the joy of your presence
> and the pleasures of living with you forever.
>
> Surely your goodness and unfailing love will
> pursue me all the days of my life, and I will live in
> the house of the Lord forever.
>
> God has reserved a priceless inheritance for his
> children. It is kept in heaven for you, pure and unde-
> filed, beyond the reach of change and decay.

"And listen now to another man, assured in his heart
that the God who sent his Son to die for us would not let
us be lost."

> Overwhelming victory is ours through Christ, who
> loved us. And I am convinced that nothing can ever
> separate us from his love. Death can't, and life can't.
> The angels can't, and the demons can't. Our fears for
> today, our worries about tomorrow, and even the
> powers of hell can't keep God's love away. Whether
> we are high above the sky or in the deepest ocean,
> nothing in all creation will ever be able to separate us

from the love of God that is revealed in Christ Jesus our Lord.

The end will come, when he will turn the Kingdom over to God the Father, having put down all enemies of every kind. For Christ must reign until he humbles all his enemies beneath his feet. And the last enemy to be destroyed is death.

Martin's uncle spoke again. "What did the Son of God himself say? Did he leave any words of assurance?"

The Traveler nodded and began to read.

"I give them eternal life, and they will never perish. No one will snatch them away from me, for my Father has given them to me, and he is more powerful than anyone else. So no one can take them from me. The Father and I are one."

The old uncle spoke again. "Traveler, when I was a child I heard stories about heaven. Long ago I dismissed them, every one, believing they were mere tales told to amuse or to bewilder. Somehow, now—I cannot explain it—I am so weary of this world, yet not certain that the next will be better. I pray it is more than a replica of this one."

The Traveler replied, "In the eyes of this world you have done well. Many who envy your position would wish to continue such an existence through all eternity. Yet you would not?" The Traveler was being kind and cruel, with kindness at the fore.

Stung by his words, but not angry, the old man said, "Is there in The Book a picture of heaven, an image we can fix our minds on?"

"Are you longing to hear stories from your childhood again?" the Traveler asked. "What can it mean to you, hearing airy fantasies now, you who have succeeded by this world's standards? Are you not an adult?"

The old man sighed, not mindful now of the fear of appearing undignified. "I am an old man, tired, pacing on from one day to the next like a gathering of ashes that have almost cooled. Nothing matters now except the Truth. Nothing matters to one with his foot slipping on the edge of eternity, nothing except what endures."

As the Traveler began to read again, Martin moved through the crowd to stand at his uncle's side.

The time will come when all the earth will be filled, as the waters fill the sea, with an awareness of the glory of the Lord.

Your eyes will see the king in all his splendor, and you will see a land that stretches into the distance.

I saw the holy city, the new Jerusalem, coming down from God out of heaven like a beautiful bride prepared for her husband.

I heard a loud shout from the throne, saying,

"Look, the home of God is now among his people! He will live with them, and they will be his people. God himself will be with them. He will remove all of their sorrows, and there will be no more death or sorrow or crying or pain. For the old world and its evils are gone forever."

The city was pure gold, as clear as glass. The wall of the city was built on foundation stones inlaid with twelve gems. The twelve gates were made of pearls— each gate from a single pearl! And the main street was pure gold, as clear as glass.

Some of the listeners laughed to themselves, for they dismissed it all as tales told by dreamers who had failed in this world. But not all laughed. Some, though they knew the Valley had its beauties, were dazzled by these pictures of something more beautiful. Then the Traveler continued to read.

No temple could be seen in the city, for the Lord God Almighty and the Lamb are its temple. And the city has no need of sun or moon, for the glory of God illuminates the city, and the Lamb is its light. The nations of the earth will walk in its light, and the rulers of the world will come and bring their glory to it.

No longer will anything be cursed. For the throne of God and of the Lamb will be there, and his servants will worship him. And they will see his face, and his name will be written on their foreheads. And there will be no night there—no need for lamps or sun—for the Lord God will shine on them. And they will reign forever and ever.

Martin had never seen his uncle shed a single tear, and as he looked now at his craggy face, so seared and worn, he wondered if those dry, gray eyes could ever bring forth tears. Yet one trickled in a meandering way down his leathery cheek. Martin was not sure what the tear was for—perhaps for remorse, perhaps for a remembrance of a sunnier day years ago when tales of heaven could be easily believed, perhaps for joy at believing now that the tales were more than tales. Martin lightly touched his uncle's arm. The old man turned to him, his lips moving slightly as though a thought had not yet formed itself into words.

The Unknown Traveler looked intently at Martin and his uncle. Then he stared for a moment at a page in the open Book, finally closing it. His eyes met those of a small boy, and though no word was spoken, the child knew what the Traveler wanted. He stepped forward and held out his arms, and the Traveler gently placed The Book in them. He placed a hand on the child's head and looked into his wide, quizzical eyes. "Little one, remember this: The Book must not go unread. Tell that to your father and your mother, and when you are a man, remember it, and teach it to your children and to their children." Then he addressed the People of the Valley for the last time.

"People of the Valley, I will leave this place in the morning. Go to your homes. It is late in the day. Remember to remember. Do not forget that I came here, but if you do, at least do not forget The Book. It is yours, as it belongs to everyone in every place." Then the Traveler spoke these words from The Book.

> Since we are receiving a Kingdom that cannot be destroyed, let us be thankful and please God by worshiping him with holy fear and awe.

The People of the Valley began to make their quiet way homeward. No one was left in the square except Martin and his uncle and the Traveler. Suddenly a night-hawk shuttled by in its angular flight and signaled to all that it was dusk.

The Traveler said, "Martin, I will abide under your roof tonight and will leave early."

Martin nodded, then turned his gaze on the old man, who in turn looked at the Traveler. The Traveler smiled slightly, and the old man, whose face still showed the track where the tear had traversed down, turned to Martin and spoke in a whisper. "Such a day, nephew. I have so much I wish to talk about with you."

Then the Traveler placed his hand on the old man's

shoulder and said in a voice not much louder than the breeze, "Remember these words of the Son of God."

> Come to me, all of you who are weary and carry heavy burdens, and I will give you rest. Take my yoke upon you. Let me teach you, because I am humble and gentle, and you will find rest for your souls. For my yoke fits perfectly, and the burden I give you is light.

The
TRAVELER
DEPARTS
The
VALLEY

WHEN MORNING broke, spilling its rose and lavender haze over the sleeping Valley, the Unknown Traveler walked to the hill on which he had had his first view of the Valley. He shivered a bit in the morning cool and gathered his coat around him. As he stood looking down on the rooftops of the Valley, he saw a lone figure running toward him, waving anxiously. It was Martin.

"Wait, Traveler! You mustn't leave without giving us all a good farewell!"

The Traveler smiled. Martin's face was flushed. It was clear that he had run all the way from his house.

"Ah, Martin, you did not need to disturb your sleep on my account. I told you last night that I would leave quietly."

"We owe you so much. I do hate to have you leave us."

The Traveler stretched out his hand and gripped Martin's shoulder, which was shivering under his dressing gown. "Friend, you owe me nothing. Whatever is of value in this bent world is owing to Almighty God. If you honor anyone, honor him. You need not even remember me. Only remember that great treasure you have, The Book. Nothing would please me more than that."

"May I walk with you awhile?"

"You are hardly dressed, Martin. It is a chilly dawn, and I must be going. I have people to see. There is so much to be done."

Martin looked into the incorruptible brown eyes of the Traveler. "Yes—yes, I am sure you do. There are so many others who don't know—or who have forgotten—the Truth." Then Martin did something that surprised himself: he extended his arms and embraced the Traveler. And the Traveler held him tightly before speaking again.

"Go home, Martin," the Unknown Traveler said in a mild voice. "Go home, and warm yourself, and live in love, and cling to the Truth like a burr clinging to your sleeve in summer. Cling to it, live for it, share it, die in it, rest in it." And with those words the Traveler released Martin and hastened down the hill, hardly leaving tracks on the silvery mantle of frost.

Martin turned and ran back to the Valley, his eyes

fixed on the smoke curling from the chimney that he knew was his. He could not remember when his senses had been so roused by the sight and sound and texture of morning. And as his feet skimmed over frosted pebbles, he was glad he could watch a day be born.

At the foot of the hill the Traveler turned, glad to see that Martin had gone home. He paused for a moment, leaning against his walking stick. Thinking of the People of the Valley, he wished for a moment that he might say to each of them these words he knew from The Book:

My dear brothers and sisters, be strong and steady, always enthusiastic about the Lord's work, for you know that nothing you do for the Lord is ever useless.

And while he paused he prayed that the People of the Valley might awaken every morning and sing the song written in The Book:

Holy, holy, holy is the Lord Almighty! The whole earth is filled with his glory!"
Bless the one who comes in the name of the Lord! Praise God in highest heaven!

A
NOTE
TO THE
READER

WHEN THE Unknown Traveler is reciting the words of
"The Book," he is, of course, quoting the words of the
Bible. The version used here is *The Book*—that is, The
New Living Translation.

The author of *Secrets from The Book* chose to weave
together Bible passages that relate to the subjects in each
chapter. People who are not familiar with the Bible—and
many who are familiar with it—often find it puzzling to
read, since its teachings on specific subjects are widely
separated across its many pages. One of the purposes of
Secrets from The Book is to help organize the Bible's teachings on the topics most crucial for living the spiritual life.
In organizing these passages and in writing the story of the
Unknown Traveler and the People of the Valley, the

author chose to focus not so much on theological doctrines as on ethical teachings. The "secrets" are not theological mysteries, but, rather, guidelines for living.

The process of weaving together related Bible passages is not new. In fact, in the early centuries of Christianity, it was a commonly-used method of teaching Christians what the Bible said on particular subjects. In a day when the few manuscripts that existed were slowly copied by hand and copies of the Bible were scarce, believers could not always have access to the Bible, so they had to learn it by heart. By memorizing these *catenae* (Latin for "chains") of Bible passages, believers could help themselves remember divine teaching on important subjects, many of which are covered in the book you are now holding.

References to the particular chapters and verses in the Bible were not included. It was felt that including these references in the text would interrupt the flow of the words. Some readers may wish to locate the passages in the Bible. For help in doing this, Bible references—chapters and verses—are listed here by the page numbers on which they are quoted in this book.

The People of the Valley

Finding The Book

ABOUT the AUTHOR

J. STEPHEN LANG is the author of twenty books, most of them dealing with the Bible. He has published his devotional prose and poetry in numerous Christian periodicals, including *Moody Magazine*, *Discipleship Journal*, *Christian History*, *Home Life*, *Liguorian*, and *The Upper Room*.

In his best-selling *Complete Book of Bible Trivia* (Tyndale House, 1988), he focused on the lighter aspects of the Bible, its many fascinating details of character and incident. In this book he shifts the focus to the more serious, life-affecting aspects of biblical truth, the great themes rather than the small details. Commenting on the difference between the two books, the author stated, "The first book was intended to be a book of facts. This is intended to be a book of insight."

He holds the B.A. in Bible and theology (Scarritt College) and the M.A. in communications (Wheaton College).